SHOULD WE GO EXTINCT?

SHOULD WE GO EXTINCT?

A Philosophical Dilemma
for Our Unbearable Times

TODD MAY

CROWN
NEW YORK

Library of Congress Cataloging-in-Publication Data
Names: May, Todd, 1955– author. Title: Should we go extinct? : a philosophical
dilemma for our unbearable times / Todd May.
Identifiers: LCCN 2024012190 | ISBN 9780593798720 (hardback) |
ISBN 9780593798737 (ebook)
Subjects: LCSH: Philosophical anthropology. | Nihilism (Philosophy) | Human
beings—Extinction—Philosophy. | Humanistic ethics. | Posthumanism.
Classification: LCC BD450 .M3345 2024 | DDC 128—dc23/eng/20240412
LC record available at https://lccn.loc.gov/2024012190

Hardcover ISBN 978-0-593-79872-0
Ebook ISBN 978-0-593-79873-7

Printed in the United States of America on acid-free paper

9 8 7 6 5 4 3 2 1

First Edition

Book design by Aubrey Khan
Earth art on pages i, iii, and vii by Shutterstock.com/Maria Yakunina

Contents

SHOULD

WE   GO

EXTINCT?

Introduction

by Michael Schur

THE BEST PHILOSOPHY IS PRACTICAL. Abstraction is great when you're in college and your only job is to sit around with your friends, pontificating and musing and babbling and exploring the limits of your own mind. But the world, someone once said, is too much with us. As we come to understand things a bit better, the problems endemic to merely existing on Earth demand examination. That examination, in turn, can lead us to some disturbing conclusions—like, just as one example, that humans kind of stink.

Many of us have at one time or another had the thought that this planet would be better off if we, collectively, weren't on it. Maybe you were standing at the South Rim of the Grand Canyon, watching a California condor glide over the Colorado River. Perhaps you were frozen in reverential silence as a herd of endangered African bush elephants splashed water on each other to cool down. Or maybe you just witnessed a guy with a mullet chug a hard cider on the back of a Jet Ski and then toss the bottle into the lake where it hit an unsuspecting duck. *We ruin everything*, you may have thought. (Honestly, with respect to our impact on the natural world, there isn't really a counter-argument.) The question is, what's to be done about it? Should humans really not exist?! How do we go about asking a question like that in earnest, much less *answering* it?

Pause for a second, and travel back with me to 2016. Because that year, I had something of a "philosophical emergency."

It had nothing to do with my life (thankfully) but rather a TV show I created called *The Good Place*, which chronicled the adventures of four deeply flawed people as they attempted to work out what it meant to be a "good" person. In the show's first season—spoiler alert, I suppose, though it's been almost a decade so really this is on you—the four humans realized that what had been sold to them as an eternal, paradisical reward for their morally pure lives on Earth was actually a twisted version of Sartre's *No Exit*—a hell of their own making, in which they were unknowingly torturing each other in various subtle ways. The architect of this prison was Michael, a demon posing as an angel. But after his plot was foiled and the show moved into its second season, Michael presented the writing staff with a seemingly insolvable philosophical problem.

The humans had improved themselves through the study of ethics and moral philosophy. In the second season, Michael now needed to do the same thing. But how? Can an immortal being even learn ethics? What possible effect could Aristotle have on a being of pure evil? And most important, if we couldn't answer these questions, had the writers written ourselves into a corner? I remember asking (pleading) out loud: Has anyone ever, somehow, written a piece of philosophy about the theoretical effect of moral reasoning on immortal beings? An answer in the affirmative seemed unlikely. But it turns out, someone had. A philosopher named Todd May. He'd written a whole book about it.

It was called, simply enough, *Death*. Reading the book led me to talk to Todd directly, and he became something akin to a philosophical advisor for the run of the show (he even appeared in our series finale, playing himself). We would call him when we got stuck in some dense ethical thicket, and he always guided us through it with patience and humor. Our conversations over the years (both related to the show and a book I myself wrote, with his help) led me to believe that there was no aspect of moral philosophy that Todd found unpleasant to think about—again, he wrote a book called *Death*—and no question he found uninteresting. So I was amused, but not surprised, when he told me his latest book was called *Should We Go Extinct?*

What do we want from our philosophical advisors? I suppose *intelligence* would be nice—they should know more than we do, certainly, or else what's the point? But with knowledge often comes condescension, or at least that sort of cold remove that often accompanies academic writing. We in the terrestrial world of real life and real problems don't take kindly to upturned noses, so we'd also want our

PA's to be *humble*, or perhaps *conversational*. We'd also like them to be *ambitious*, to attack and dissect the sorts of issues that cause us sleepless nights and lurk around the dark corners of our consciousness. Last, we'd like them to be *humane*, or more simply, *friendly*. That's not an adjective often applied to academic philosophers, but if we're signing up for pedagogy, it would be nice if we felt our teacher were on our side. Rooting for us. Invested in the outcomes at which we arrive, and adept at illuminating the paths we take along the way.

All of this is why Todd was the perfect advisor for us and is the ideal person to write this particular book. There aren't many questions bigger than "Should we, you know, exist?" Answering "Yes, we should" seems facile, and ignores our undeniably horrifying impact on the planet. Answering "No, we shouldn't" is, you know . . . kind of bleak. And regardless of the answer, a question like this in the wrong hands could be unpleasant to merely contemplate. We might be subjected to a steely Kantian, searching for some maxim we can follow and ignoring the issue's emotional component. Or worse: we may suffer at the hands of a cold utilitarian lost in the calculus of the question, or some other pedagogical technician making arguments so intricate and theoretical that the very guts of the question at hand are buried under an avalanche of blather. But Todd, whom I know to be a humble, conversational, ambitious, and deeply human thinker, both takes the question seriously and walks us patiently through the arguments for and against. (It helps that he's quite funny. Chapter one ends with this sentence:

"And with that, let's dig in to the question of whether humanity should continue." Which made me genuinely laugh, and trust me, he meant it to.) The question is alarming. The person asking it is calm and kind.

Ask the biggest questions. Tease out the answers. Do it warmly, thoughtfully, and humanely. This is the job of the philosopher. For more than five years, Todd May was my philosophical advisor. I heartily recommend that he be yours as well.

A Disturbing Question

I T'S THREE IN THE MORNING—3:12 to be exact. You know this because you just checked. Again. What are you thinking about at this time of night? You're thinking about the climate crisis, even though you might not call it that. You're thinking about the floods you just read about in the Midwest. Or maybe the one in New York. You're thinking about the fires in California. Or the ones in Greece. You're thinking about the recent tornado watch where you live—in a place that never has tornados.

Your mind turns to the war in Ukraine and to Vladimir Putin, who's threatening to use nuclear weapons on the Ukrainian people (not to mention his underling Dmitry Medvedev, who's out there threatening to nuke *everyone*). Will that happen? Should you prepare? How would you even do that?

Then your thoughts take another step. The climate crisis. Nuclear weapons. *We* did that. Humanity did it. It wasn't some other species that rose up and ordered us to destroy the planet. We did all this. It's our fault.

If the animals of the planet, concerned for the collapse of their environment and the possibility of nuclear annihilation, were able to have a convention to judge us, you realize, we would not fare so well. They would likely condemn us to the extinction we are visiting upon so many of them.

At that point, though, you think, hey, it's three in the morning and if you don't get any sleep, then work tomorrow is not going to go so well. Plus, an animal convention? That's pretty crazy. Turn over and get some rest.

But really, though, it is that crazy? Not the animal convention: That *is* crazy. But the idea that humans are destroying life on the planet for many of our fellow creatures or that we could get into a war that would make life unlivable for many others—that's not so crazy. Instead, it's fact. And how about the thought that given what we're doing, perhaps we should seriously consider whether we should go extinct, whether the world would be better off without us? Maybe that's not so crazy either.

The not-craziness of it is why I've been thinking about this for some time now. In fact, several years ago I penned some very preliminary thoughts on it for the (now extinct) *New York Times* blog *The Stone,* raising the possibility that human extinction might be at once a tragedy and a good thing. It would be a tragedy for two reasons. First, in addition to the suffering that would precede it, it would involve the loss of much of what humans value and only humans can create: art, science, and so on. Second—here is the classically tragic part—that loss would be caused by humans. We, like King Lear or Oedipus, would be the cause of our demise.

But our extinction would not be all bad news. The end of human existence would also be the end of the massive suffering humans cause, largely to non-human animals. (Granted, we also cause a good bit of suffering to one another—and not just through social media. But, as I'll argue in the next chapter, for most of us our lives, in the end, are well worth living.) It's not that animals don't cause suffering to one another. Of course they do. But no non-human animal can cause the extraordinary level of suffering that humans do, through factory farming and the consumption that goes along with it, deforestation, plastic disposal into the oceans, scientific experimentation, and the like.

The emerging climate crisis, coupled with the Russian invasion of Ukraine and the nuclear threats that have gone with it, started me thinking about that article again. I recognized that there was a lot more that needed to be said. I hadn't argued that our exit from the planetary scene would *definitely* be good, although at the time prominent thinkers on the extreme right accused me of that.* In several places in the piece, I noted complications that would have to be considered more fully in order to sort the issue out in proper

---

* (All of which led to the predictable right-wing trolling of my email account for several days, with almost all of the emails offering some version of "Why don't you go extinct?" There must be an office, like the ones that create the messages for fortune cookies, that generates stock responses to public statements that offend the far right.)

detail. It was those complications that started me thinking again. In light of a possible nuclear conflagration or, more likely, increasing environmental devastation, I began to think it might be worthwhile to revisit in a more sustained way the question of whether the end of humanity would ultimately be a good thing.

Most folks assume our extinction would be a bad thing. They may not be wrong. But they also may not be right. What I hope to offer here, by lingering over that question from different angles, is a set of reflections at the extreme of human existence that can enlighten our thoughts about who and where we are and where we might or might not— and ought and ought not to—be headed.

What Are We Actually Asking Here?

To begin, I want to distinguish the reflections here from another set of reflections that might, at a glance, be confused with it. After all, there is a lot of talk and writing about extinction and near-extinction these days. That talk and those writings, often referring to "climate anxiety" or "climate grief," involve lamentations about our climate crisis and the future it may hold for our children and grandchildren, and increasingly for us.

Climate anxiety and climate grief are not the same thing, but they are related. Climate anxiety concerns the psychological state of worry about what's happening to the environment and what it portends for the future—in general future generations but often more particularly the future of those a person cares about. All of us know young people who are either anxious about whether to bring the next generation into the world or have decided definitely not to do so. They have come to the entirely reasonable conclusion that the climate crisis is only going to worsen and that the world they would be bringing their kids into will in all likelihood be, at best, environmentally challenging for them. After all, the effects of the climate crisis are backloaded; what we're experiencing now is the result of previous emissions. Current emissions are going to compound present ills with others that are more powerful and more dangerous than what we're experiencing now. Moreover, even if we stopped our greenhouse gas emissions today—this very day—we could not prevent those worsening effects.

Climate grief is a little further along from climate anxiety. If climate anxiety is concern for what will happen, climate grief is a form of sorrow for it. It accepts the inevitability of climate devastation and proactively grieves for it. After all, it might be argued, if there is going to be a general human demise, we had better start grieving now since there may not be a lot of us left to grieve afterward.

In any event, our reflections here lie in a certain sense beneath these concerns. Both climate anxiety and climate grief assume that human extinction or something like it would be a bad thing (or at least a sad thing, even if in our darkest moments at three a.m. we might think it an appropriate thing). It is that assumption that I would like to put under the microscope.[*]

Of course, sooner or later, all species go extinct. We're not likely to be exceptions to this. And so one might say, if we're going to go extinct anyway, why should we even be concerned with the question of whether we should? Why raise the question at all?

Granted, there is no reason to think that humans, even in the long term, will avoid extinction. However, that inescapability leaves two big moral questions unanswered. First, should we go extinct sooner rather than later? Would it be better to take our leave within a generation or two rather than put it off for centuries or eons from now? The next two chapters will tackle this.

The other big moral question is this: If there is at least some reason to think it would be better if we went extinct, is there anything we can do to mitigate that? Could we do more to justify our continuing existence on the planet? That is the focus of the book's final chapter.

How Might Extinction Occur?

If we're going to confront the question of whether it's okay to continue our species, one of the first things we'll want to

---

[*] And even if someone were to decide that human extinction would be a good thing, climate anxiety or grief would not be inappropriate. There is no necessary conflict between the two. After all, I can believe that some relative of mine was a terrible person and that their death made the world a little better off while at the same time grieving that death.

do is to get a grip on how that extinction—if it were to occur—might happen. There are many different scenarios to consider, some more realistic than others. (In his comprehensive history of thought about extinction, *Human Extinction: A History of the Science and Ethics of Annihilation*, Émile Torres canvases a number of them.) But not all extinctions are the same. Some of them would have consequences that would be disastrous far beyond humans, and so they're not worth considering by way of moral calculus. Others are more complex.

We have already mentioned two possible scenarios: the climate crisis and nuclear annihilation. Nuclear annihilation is probably not suitable for our purposes. (Actually, it's not suitable for a lot of purposes.) The problem is that it's too broadly destructive. The kind of nuclear catastrophe that would be pervasive enough to destroy humanity (or nearly destroy it—more on near-destruction in a bit) would also annihilate many other forms of life at the same time. The radiation from a nuclear holocaust would cause a massive die-off of all kinds of life and, moreover, would make it difficult for life to flourish for many decades, and even centuries, to come. Basically, if we went out this way, any benefit our disappearance would have for other living beings would be largely canceled out by our taking most of those beings with us. It'd be one final kiss-off from us to the rest of life. This isn't to say there aren't plenty of excellent reasons to ponder over the prospect of a nuclear cataclysm, or to worry about its occurrence; it's just that it's not much help in thinking about the morality of continued human existence.

How about the climate crisis, then? That, it seems to me, is closer to what we should consider. But it's not exactly there. While a climate crisis that would eliminate human existence would, for sure, eliminate a number of other species along the way (in particular species that we have domesticated), it would leave room for many of the existing species either to evolve or bounce back in population. So that's a plus. And it would end the threat of continued environmental degradation by the one species that specializes in fostering such degradation. On the other hand, the climate crisis will affect other species as well, both directly and indirectly through its effect on the ecosystems in which these species exist. We already see some of the effects of the crisis on other species, from collapsing populations of various species of fish to the bleaching of coral reefs to the demise of the ice sheets necessary for polar bear life.

A third possibility, one that has recently caught some folks' attention, is a worldwide pandemic that affected humans more than other species. Although Covid currently seems to be under some control, there is no reason not to think that another virus might catch us unawares, and the next one—or the one after—might be harder to contain.

Perhaps one of the cleanest scenarios for our purposes is the most far-fetched, but worth a moment of discussion just because it is so clean. It's what we might call the *Children of Men* scenario, after the novel and subsequent movie of that name. The plot of *Children of Men* begins—before all the action takes place—in a world of infertility. Men's sperm count has dropped to zero and with it the prospect of human extinction has arisen. Although I have heard that the toxins in our environment are reducing men's sperm count, the full *Children of Men* scenario seems a bit of a stretch, at least at the moment.

We could look at still other scenarios, but they are likely to be close to one of the four we've considered here. For instance, we could imagine a world of diminishing resources in which humans are in continuous violent conflicts over basic necessities until there's nobody left to fight. But that seems more likely a scenario we would see at the end of the climate crisis, a sort of working out of the climate crisis endgame, rather than a distinct scenario in its own right. Finally, there is the entirely realistic scenario of eventual planetary destruction through the gradual expansion of the sun. That, of course, is going to happen and with it will come the extinction of the human species, assuming (probably unrealistically) that we would last that long. However, since that will also involve the extinction of every other species, it doesn't really offer much to consider in the way of assessing the benefits and drawbacks of human disappearance.

How About Just a Smaller Population?

At this point, you may have a reservation to put forward. On any realistic scenario aside from—and perhaps including— a nuclear cataclysm, there seems no reason to believe that humans will be entirely eliminated. Rather than human extinction, aren't we more likely to have a kind of human marginalization? There will be humans, but in small bands that are remote from one another and perhaps unlikely to be in communication. Isn't that more probable than complete human extinction under the scenarios we're considering?

This is an important reservation, one that we will return to in the following chapters, but let me offer an initial response here. First, there is a reservation I have about the reservation itself. Suppose that humans did not go extinct but rather existed in small groups scattered around. It seems likely that eventually they would find one another, build up larger communities, and then revisit a human history similar to the one we've already been through so that sooner or later we'd find ourselves in the same place we're at now—or at least one close enough. Sustaining larger communities requires agriculture, which leads to even larger communities, which require more food, which is likely to lead to factory farming and industrialization and air travel and overconsumption, and then we're off and running to another climate crisis as well as other forms of environmental degradation.

However, suppose that didn't happen. Suppose there were just small groups of humans that continued to exist separate from one another and living in a sustainable way, much as indigenous ethnic groups did in the U.S. before the Europeans arrived. I take it that this scenario would be what we might call a "friendly amendment" to the scenario of extinction. Although this would not be possible under a true *Children of Men* schema, a full scenario of that sort is very unlikely. On the basis of a climate catastrophe, though, there is at least some reason to believe that there would be small groups of people still living, and if they were to take on the lessons of sustainable food production and environmental guardianship—basically, the lessons that Europeans did not take on the first time around from the indigenous groups we slaughtered—then it is possible to imagine the continuation of the species over the longer term. How much the difference between extinction and the continuation of humanity at a much smaller scale would matter will occupy us a bit as we go along.

What About Mass Human Suicide?

When I've talked to people about the possibility of human extinction, everyone always asks, "Well, if it turns out our extinction would be so great, then why not speed it up? What about mass human suicide?" (By "everyone," I mean the few conversationally charitable people I actually bring this up with.) If, they ask, we currently existing humans are causing such destruction—and we are—then shouldn't we also ask about whether humanity should just end itself at this moment, without waiting for the climate crisis or some other cataclysm to do the work for us?

Here's the thing, though. Even if we were to conclude (and I'm not saying we will) that it would be good for humanity to end, the prospect of mass human suicide is very different *morally* from the kind of extinction we've been considering here, for at least two reasons. First, to ask people to end their lives is, on almost any moral accounting, requesting too profound a sacrifice. (And would, rightfully, be frowned upon.) To be sure, there are rare situations where one might think that it would be good for a person to end their life. Most parents, I think, would end their lives in order to save the lives of their children. Many people would and do sacrifice their lives for a cause or an ideal or a country they believe in. As I write these lines, people in Ukraine are resisting a horrific invasion by Russia. Many Ukrainians have willingly sacrificed their lives for those they care about as well as for the sake of the continued existence of their country. We might admire that, but it doesn't seem in most cases that we should hold people to it. Further, to ask people to end their lives, or more pointedly to say that people have some *obligation* to end their lives in order not to burden the environment or to help save non-human animal life—well, it places a moral onus on folks that is beyond what most of us think reasonable.

It is one thing to say, prompted by environmental degradation and animal suffering, that further human life should not come into existence. This does not cause trouble for that further life. Why not? For the straightforward reason that there isn't somebody there waiting to come into existence. There isn't someone in particular, say Fred, who is waiting in the wings for someone to conceive him but who won't come into existence because he won't be conceived. Human extinction, in that sense, is not a loss for anyone who would not be born, since there isn't anybody in particular who would not be born. No Fred, no foul. However, suicide—as you might already be thinking—is a great loss for most of us who are already in existence.

Moreover, in a scenario where we ask currently existing humans to sacrifice themselves, we would also know that our friends and loved ones are losing their lives. This is as bad, and in some ways worse, than asking for personal suicide. (You may be thinking of certain people at family gatherings whom you consider exceptions to this. I'll leave that to your conscience.) Imagine that you were asked to end your life, not for the sake of those you love, but instead alongside them? That is very different from personal sacrifice. The fact that you would be told that the sacrifice of all human beings would be really good for other living beings and a variety of ecosystems doesn't do the job of justifying the abandonment of lives that are currently engaged with the world and with one another.

One Way Not to Approach Our Question

Having ruled out mass suicide—whew!—how should we approach the question of whether it would be better if humans were to go extinct? In order to clear the ground, let me first offer a way in which we're *not* going to approach the question. It's worth spending a moment on, since it's a tempting way to frame the issues, and it will be easy to confuse it with what I think is the best approach.

We are not asking whether human beings *deserve* to go extinct. The rough idea behind that question would be this: We humans have, over the course of our recent history, done immense damage to non-human life. Through the related activities of overpopulation, factory farming, plastic production, greenhouse gas emissions, scientific experimentation on animal bodies, and so on, we have violated any moral permission we might have to continue our existence on the planet. We are responsible for what we have done, and since the only adequate way to punish us for this is to end our continued existence, human extinction is the proper retribution for us.

The problem with this way of approaching the issue is that it is not correct to say that all of humanity is responsible for the environmental degradation associated with our species. In fact, most human beings are only minimally responsible for the harm that has been done to other living beings and ecosystems. Just as the problem associated with possible nuclear annihilation can be traced back to (as well as currently associated with) a certain group of white Europeans and Americans, mostly male, so the climate crisis and related environmental disasters are largely the product of people in Europe and people of European descent. Moreover, it is a subset of people of European descent to whom the responsibility largely falls. We usually punish people for something they've done to deserve punishment. But most people—particularly in developing countries—have done very little if anything to contribute to the climate crisis. Why should they deserve extinction?

Yet although the root of environmental problems lies in a relatively small group among the human population, ultimately the sheer number and consequent aggregate consumption of human beings pose a threat to the existence and flourishing of other living beings and their ecosystems.

While it is true that, individually, most humans contribute very little to the difficulties that raise the moral question of human extinction, collectively we pose an enormous threat.

So then, even if humans don't *deserve* to go extinct as a species, wouldn't the consequences of our going extinct be better? That's the question we're asking: Given all the damage we do to the environment and all the pain we cause to our fellow creatures, wouldn't the elimination of our species bring about *a better outcome* than our continuing to propagate and exist?

A Second, Somewhat but Not Always Entirely Helpful Way to Approach Our Question

One of the most important theories in moral philosophy is utilitarianism. It's a helpful theory for thinking about lots of moral issues, and we'll definitely use it in the chapters to come. But it tends to be overly simplistic when confronted with complicated moral dilemmas like the one we're sorting out here, so we need to be careful. Let me explain.

Utilitarianism stems from the philosophical work of the eighteenth-century thinker Jeremy Bentham, followed up in the nineteenth century by John Stuart Mill. Bentham's idea was that the morally right act to commit was the one that caused the most pleasure. He had ways of measuring pleasure, which we really don't need to linger over (they're not creepy, just complex . . . okay, they're sometimes a little weird), but the goal was more pleasure—or, more precisely, more pleasure over pain. For Bentham, there was a single scale of well-being, that of pleasure, and all the good aspects of a life could be accounted for on that scale. The right way to approach morality would be to ask which act would create the most pleasure over pain—or, in more unfortunate situations, the least pain—and to perform that act.

Should animals count in the calculus? Here, Bentham was way ahead of his own time, and to some extent ours. He believed that animal pain and pleasure *should* count, just as human pain and pleasure should. Most philosophers up until recently largely discounted the suffering of non-human animals as a moral matter, but Bentham rejected that idea. His view was that what mattered morally was not reason but pleasure and pain. In his most often cited words, "The question is not, Can they reason?, nor Can they talk? but, Can they suffer? Why should the law refuse its protection to any sensitive being?"

Mill sided with Bentham on the idea that what matters is pain and pleasure, but added a detail that brought back the privilege to human beings, and even to a subset of human beings. He thought that there were two types of pleasures, higher and lower ones. The higher ones were better and of a different quality from the lower ones. In his view, a person who had the opportunity would always choose a higher pleasure over a lower one.

Mill's distinction between higher and lower pleasures puts non-human animals in a bad spot. After all, they can't experience the pleasure of either opera or baseball, so their preferences aren't going to account for much. Mill himself seems to endorse this view when he writes, "It is better to be a human being dissatisfied than a pig satisfied; better to be Socrates dissatisfied than a fool satisfied. And if the fool, or the pig, are of a different opinion, it is because they only know their own side of the question." (Socrates, right? The dissatisfied philosopher as the model of the highest form of happiness.)

The traditional utilitarianism of Bentham and Mill gives us one or two simple scales of measuring consequences, both of which have to do with a single good to be promoted: pleasure. But is this really adequate for our purposes? Isn't it instead a bit too crude a tool to employ in asking whether the consequences of continued human existence are worth the pain and suffering we cause? Consider this.

Let's assume for a moment that we can measure the amount of suffering we inflict on other animals. Even if we can't put a specific number on it, we know that it is enormous. Billions of animals are raised each year for human consumption, and most of them live short, painful lives under horrific conditions. Suppose we could measure that, broadly speaking. What would we place on the other side of the scale, the pleasurable things that would tilt the balance? How would we measure the value of the existence of science and literature, opera and baseball? Although Mill might be mistaken in posing a simple hierarchy of higher and lower pleasures, he is surely seeing something: Not all consequences can be readily reduced to the single scale that Bentham used.

What's more, and more disturbing about traditional utilitarianism, is that if we were to use a simple scale like the one Bentham suggests, we might find ourselves returning to the question of mass human suicide as a moral possibility. After all, suppose all the pain that we cause the billions of other living animals through factory farming, ecosystem devastation, the dumping of plastic into the oceans, and our contribution to the climate crisis—suppose we were to measure all that against the pain of mass human suicide. It's actually not at all clear that the sum total of our pain would outweigh the sum total of the pain we cause to other living beings. Or, looked at from the other side, suppose we were all to eliminate ourselves as painlessly as possible. How much pain would that cause, and how much suffering would that save current and future animals from having to endure our practices of factory farming and so on?*

A utilitarian could say that the reason there would be less animal suffering if we all ended our existence is that the animal lives that would otherwise have come into existence through our practices—and the suffering they would experience—will not do so. And the animals that do come into existence would generally be better off. If we go extinct, so goes the microplastic in fish guts, the destruction of the Amazonian rain forest and its inhabitants, the decline

---

* We need to be a little careful here in talking about "future animals." There is no such thing as a particular future animal, just as there are no particular future human beings. (Remember Fred?) There are animals that will exist in the future. But there is no such thing at this moment as a "future animal." Just as there was no particular you that existed as a future you before your parental behavior created you, there are no particular animals that occupy the category "future animals."

of Arctic ice that starves polar bears, and perhaps most egregious of all, the agony of billions of factory-farmed cows and pigs and chickens.

All of this is not to argue that a traditional utilitarian view isn't helpful for us. As we'll see, it will be quite important at points. But we can't rest our reflections on utilitarianism alone. So while we will use utilitarianism in our considerations, it won't be as the overarching framework. If we're going to approach the question of human extinction, we will need a more versatile approach. We need to take what philosophers often call a "pluralist" view. Pluralism recognizes that moral goodness and badness come in different forms and so require different perspectives if we're adequately to grasp all of what's at stake. This more nuanced approach will help us to see our existence and what matters about it in a more richly articulated way.

Who's Asking the Question?

Before turning to that task, however, there is one more framing idea we should discuss. It offers a fresh set of complications, so what I offer here is just a quick sketch of the contours. We'll fill it in more later on.

The point is this: The questions we're asking here and, more important, the moral reflections prompted by them, are coming from a human viewpoint. This might seem obvious. But the implications of it may not be.

First, our assessment of the experiences of non-human animals—their pain and pleasure or their attachment to life—can only come from a human interpretation of their behavior. We can't ask them what they're feeling or experiencing. (Well, we can. But it's hard to get a duck to tell you how it really feels about being alive.) This is inevitable. It might seem like an exercise in "human-centrism," but we really have no alternative. If we're going to ask at all about our treatment of and relationship to other animals, we're going to have to do it from our own standpoint. The alternative is not to consider our moral relationships with our fellow creatures at all.

Here's something else to think about: If I'm pondering what a world might be like without humans, I might consider something like the beauty of a natural environment. That beauty presents itself to me, as a human. So what do I make of the fact that there is something that a human would recognize as beautiful and that still exists but without any humans to recognize its beauty? This is a conundrum we'll develop in the third chapter.

It might seem that I'm being a bit blithe when it comes to the idea of the "human" perspective. After all, aren't there many perspectives within the human, and so many different ways to approach the question of whether we should go extinct? Isn't it a bit presumptuous of me to pretend to speak for *the* human perspective? However, I believe that the concerns and considerations in the following chapters would be recognized as morally relevant by a broad swath of humanity. That's not to say that everyone would agree with everything I say, but instead that my perspective would be a recognizably moral one, if only one among others. So when I refer to a human perspective—or more broadly to the idea of what "we" might think—you can take it as a perspective within the human, a perspective that requires a human being in order to be considered or advanced.

And with that, let's dig in to the question of whether humanity should continue.

TWO

What's So Good
About Humanity?

LET'S GO FOR THE GOOD NEWS FIRST. After all, there are plenty of positive things we might say about humanity. Not all of humanity maybe, but certainly a lot of it. Maybe enough to tilt the balance in favor of continuing our species. Let's focus on that before we take a deep breath and look at the other side of the ledger.

When parents—at least the parents I know—think of bringing new people into the world, one of the central hopes they have for them is that they'll be happy, or at least happy enough that they consider their lives worth living. We tend to think that, with exceptions, most people's lives are worth living. So right away we seem to have some reason to bring more people into existence. I wouldn't go so far as to say that there is an *obligation* to create more people. But the fact that they might have good or decent lives is a reason in favor of doing so. (That reason can be counterbalanced by any number of other countervailing reasons, from the economic pressure of raising kids to psychological stress to just not really wanting to have kids around.)

If we pull the lens back just a bit, we might say that having people on the planet whose lives are worth living is in general a good thing—both for them and because it creates more happiness in the world than there would otherwise be. So, let the species continue!

But Is Life Really Worth Living?

Wait, what? Do we really want to consider that life might not be worth living—just when we were starting to feel good about ourselves? Who might think otherwise, except someone in terrible pain or, worse, a philosopher?

We're going to go for the second option.

The philosopher David Benatar wrote a book that's still influential among folks who think about these issues. Its title couldn't be more apt—*Better Never to Have Been*. In that book he argues two related things: that human lives are really not worth living and that we shouldn't bring new human lives into the world. That puts him in the "yes" column for human extinction. Is he right?

Benatar's argument for not bringing new human lives into the world is a bit technical, but his defense of the idea that most human lives, well, suck, is pretty straightforward. For him, the inevitability of suffering, if from no other cause than from the fact that we'll die, cancels out any pleasure or happiness we experience in the course of our existence. Add to that the various unpleasantnesses of everyday existence, from hunger and thirst to general weariness, as well as more significant experiences, from regret and resentment to the death of loves ones, and, it seems to Benatar, there will not be enough on the other side of the scale to make it all worth it.

Pretty dark. But we might ask him, if the very inevitability of suffering and death makes life not worth it, why, then, are most people so attached to their lives? Why, if you ask people whether their lives are worth living or whether they're glad they were brought into existence, will they generally offer a positive answer?

This, in Benatar's eyes, has to do with a couple of psychological principles. First, he thinks we're fooling ourselves. Most important, in his eyes, is the Pollyanna Principle— the idea people are much more optimistic about the character of their lives than their lives merit. We recall positive experiences more than negative ones, we think the future will be better than it will likely be, and so on. Benatar also points to what the philosopher Amartya Sen called "adaptive preferences"—when people adjust their preferences to fit their current circumstances. For instance, a person who lives in a remote, impoverished area is not likely to prefer being a doctor or a lawyer but instead maybe just a subsistence farmer. Being a doctor or a lawyer is not on their radar. It's not that they haven't heard about doctors or lawyers— maybe they have. Rather, it's that they adapt their preferences to what seems realistic given the situation they find themselves in.

For Benatar, adaptive preferences have an existential flair. He thinks they shield us from the painful recognition that our lives are not really very happy ones. We tell ourselves that our lives are going pretty well compared to people whose lives are much worse. We adapt to changing circumstances, like having to use a wheelchair or take medicine with side effects. We say that everything happens for the best or at least for a reason, and so what seems like a setback is actually just a lesson or a challenge to be overcome. All in all, we ignore the fact that much of our lives are actually pretty unhappy, and this shelters us from the depressing realization that human existence is, except under highly unusual circumstances, an unfortunate thing. If Benatar is right, then there is a good reason for humans to go extinct. It is wrong to bring people into the world, since they will spend much of their time deluding themselves about how badly their lives are going.

Well, that's depressing. This is supposed to be a chapter on why we *should* continue our species, and here we are questioning whether our lives are worth living in the first place. So should we accept Benatar's argument, and with it the idea that we should, to be kind to everyone who might follow us, make sure that there isn't anybody who will actually follow us?

I think there are two reasons to reject Benatar's pessimism about life. For most of us, life is just better than that. One reason involves the pluralism I've mentioned a couple of times. Benatar's view seems to me to be too superficial or "flat," much like Jeremy Bentham's view of goodness and badness as simply a matter of pleasure and pain. Benatar is at pains to reject the idea that we can just sum up happiness and unhappiness in a simple way. He points out that there are different intensities of happiness, that the order in which happiness and unhappiness take place in a life matters, as does the spread of happiness over its course, and so on. In addition, he considers several standard views of happiness: hedonistic views that consider only pleasure and pain, desire-fulfillment views that focus on people's getting what they want, and objective list theories that are concerned with getting different types of goods. In each case, he argues that the bad outweighs the good, even though most people don't recognize it. To sum up, then, there is, for Benatar, more pain than pleasure in human life, most of our desires go unfulfilled, and any objective view of our lives misses, among other things, that from the perspective of the universe our lives don't really count for much.

However, if we turn to a pluralistic view of the value of human existence, we see that there are different goods to a human life that aren't on the same scale as the pain and suffering. One type of good that's not on Benatar's radar is what I might call "meaningfulness." I think of meaningfulness as an experience that doesn't require some cosmic Meaning of Life that is out there in the universe waiting for us to discover it. Our lives can often be characterized by different themes, themes I call "narrative values." (I've written a book about this, which I won't give you the title for here, in order to stay away from self-promotion. However, if you're really interested, you can find the reference on page 151. Just saying.) For instance, some lives are lived intensely, involving deep engagement with whatever activities the person is participating in at the moment. Other lives are spiritual, committed in an ongoing way to a transcendent force or being that offers a sense of worthwhileness to those lives. Still others are intellectually curious, or spontaneous, or adventurous, or loyal. These lived themes help integrate the events—some painful, some pleasurable, some otherwise—into a pattern that can offer a person's life a sense of meaning that isn't reducible to the felt goodness or badness of particular moments or even the aggregate of them. A narrative value can make a life worth living beyond just the pain or pleasure it involves. For instance, a person with periodically debilitating depression might yet live a life of, say, steadfast loyalty to friends or dedicated spirituality that would lend that life meaning beyond the pain of the depression they endure.

There are other ways as well of thinking about our lives that lend them dimensions beyond the ones Benatar considers. But even setting these aside, I think Benatar's view can be challenged on something like its own terms. He says that most of us are mistaken about the character of our lives. We endorse them, but that is because we deceive ourselves about what they're actually like. To be sure, we deceive ourselves about many things; people are masters of self-deception. But is it fair to say that most of us are deceiving ourselves about how happy our lives are or how they are going generally?

Here's a way to think about our lives that runs counter to Benatar's view. Perhaps he has things the wrong way around: The happy or pleasurable parts or aspects of our

lives actually *do* offset the painful parts. Perhaps the Pollyanna Principle is not necessarily an inaccurate take on the
character of our lives. It might, in fact, be an accurate one.
Think of it this way: The trajectories of most human lives
include painful periods and pleasurable periods—and, of
course, moments of both at the same time, like when we
exercise vigorously or get a deep muscle massage. (In the
case of the deep muscle massage, at least in my experience,
the real pleasure lies in the moment when I realize that it's
over.) And perhaps the happy or pleasurable aspects of our
lives make the painful ones worth it, even if there are fewer
happy moments or even if they are less intense or long-
lasting. This is not just the idea that we need the painful
moments in order to enjoy the pleasurable ones. That's true
in some cases, but to be honest I'm a bit leery of the cliché
that suffering necessarily adds to the improvement of people's lives. Another way to put it would be "Yes, there has
been a lot of pain, but this happiness I'm experiencing now
makes it all worth it. If I had to go through that pain again
in order to have this experience, I would totally do it." This
is pleasure that outweighs pain, not because the pain makes
us stronger or more psychologically adept, but in a different
way. Having gone through that pain and finding this pleasure on the other side, we recognize that the pain is *less important* than the pleasure following it. And so overall the
experience is one of pleasure more than pain.

Benatar, of course, thinks this way of considering our
lives is self-deceptive, a form of an adaptive preference or an
expression of the Pollyanna Principle. But why should we

agree with him on that? Why not take our own weighing of our pain or suffering and happiness at face value? Sure, there may be times when people are wrong about their own weighing, but isn't that just a matter of specific people in specific circumstances? There doesn't seem to be any reason to say that almost everyone who weighs the pain and happiness of their lives and finds the balance in favor of happiness is mistaken.

Of course, most of us don't do this basic type of weighing. Our reflective relationship to our lives is more nuanced than that, involving a plurality of values such as narrative values. But even on the pain/happiness scale, the judgment that pleasure is worth the pain does not strike me as necessarily wrong.

Adding Happiness to the World

If this is right, then we can at least tentatively assume that most human lives are happy or pleasurable, or at least happy or pleasurable enough. Not every human life is a happy one, of course. I once met a seventeen-year-old refugee living under horrific circumstances, who told me that he berated his father for bringing him into the world, knowing what his life would be like. In general, though, we can assume that for most of us there is a balance of pleasure or happiness over unhappiness or suffering. This means, among other things, that most lives overall add a degree of happiness to the world. If we think, with the utilitarians, of happiness as a good thing—and why shouldn't we?—this means that the

existence of most human lives adds something positive to
the world that would not be there if those humans did not
exist.

So if humans add happiness to the world, that would give
us a reason to keep our species going, wouldn't it? Happiness is good, after all. Seems so. But does adding happiness
to the world actually make the world better?

It's not so cut-and-dried. Imagine two worlds, one where
there are no beings that experience either happiness or unhappiness. In this world, there are people kind of like us,
but they just go through their lives in a rote way—not depressed, but not happy either. They would be like mechani-
cal people, just doing what they needed to do with no
particular sense of happiness about their successes or suffering about their failures. Contrast that world with another
one, more like our world. In this other world, there are beings like us who experience both pain and happiness, but
the happiness generally outweighs the pain. There is a balance of happiness over pain in the lives of those in that
world. Wouldn't we be tempted to say that the second
world is better than the first one, and that the reason for
this is that there is more happiness in that second world?
On the flip side, if there were more pain than happiness,
wouldn't that tilt us more toward preferring the first world,
the rote one?

Now, someone might object here that it's not the happiness itself that makes the world better, but happy people.
It's the fact that there are people who are happy that marks
the improvement of the second world over the first one, not

just some free-floating happiness out there in the ether. We prefer that whoever is there is happy, but the happiness only has a point if it is attached to the people who exist.

This is a reasonable objection. In fact, there is an idea in philosophy, one we've seen briefly already, that reflects it. Almost all of us think that people have an obligation not to bring people into the world who they know will have miserable lives, lives that they feel would not be worth living. On the other hand, though, there is no *obligation* to bring people into the world who they know will be happy. Misery creates an obligation to refrain, but happiness does not create an obligation to reproduce.

If we were to take the view that happiness itself doesn't add anything to the world, then there are no grounds—at least on the basis of happiness—to continue humanity. Nothing is lost if we don't keep our species going. If we have any obligation at all, it's only to ensure that those who follow us are happy. There is no obligation to create any people who follow us, though. Other grounds to continue humanity might exist, some of which we'll see in a bit. But the creation of happiness, in this view, doesn't tell against human extinction. And, okay, that's a pretty reasonable view.

But there is another view, just as reasonable, that would tell in favor of our continued existence. We might put it this way: There is no obligation to bring happy people into the world, fair enough. But isn't there at least a *reason*—if not an obligation—to create happy people? Why? Well, because they would be happy. That's a good thing, yes? And if we have a reason to bring people into the world who would be happy, what is that reason? You got it—happiness. By adding happy people to the world, we've added happiness, and the world is now a little better off than it was, because there's more happiness in it.

Going in this direction would allow that the existence of happiness itself makes the world better. The utilitarians, for all their shortcomings, are onto something here. If human life is for most people one of greater happiness than pain, then the existence of human beings overall adds something good to the planet. There is a point to our not going extinct.

Of course, that happiness, as we have seen, often happens at the price of great suffering for other living creatures. Any argument for continued human existence that depends on the happiness of human beings is going to have to lay the pain we cause other animals on the other side of the scale and consider whether that tips it in the other direction, against our continued existence. We'll return to this difficulty in the next chapter. Before we go any further, though, we need to linger over the idea of human happiness for a bit. There's a complication here that we haven't yet considered.

Happiness, we have seen, makes the world better. From there we might be tempted to argue that more happiness will make the world better still. After all, if the addition of happiness is improving things, wouldn't adding more happiness offer more improvement? And if that's right, then shouldn't we be adding as many people to the world as we possibly can, as long as they have a modicum of happiness? That is, rather than going extinct, shouldn't we be doing the opposite—creating as many people as we can that might be at all happy, all in order to add more happiness to the world?

That's where things get a bit sticky. What matters is not just the amount of happiness, but how that happiness is spread around. That is, it isn't just the total amount of happiness that makes the world better, but who has more and who has less of it.

To see why, imagine two different worlds from the ones we just pondered. We'll need to put some numbers on the amount of happiness that people are experiencing in these worlds, since we're talking about more and less happiness. I know that's a little arbitrary, but it should capture the point.

In the first world, there are a million people who are thriving. They all have a good education, flourishing friendships, satisfying family lives, and jobs that stimulate them and pay a generous salary. They are in good health and play sports for fun and recreation. They prefer winning when they play but have enough perspective that when they lose they recognize they've enjoyed the experience of competition. The hours before they go to sleep are peaceful ones, and the hours after they awaken are joyous; they look forward to the day ahead. It's not that everything is always dandy. There are health problems and conflicts and occasional injuries. And, since these are mortal beings, they all face death. But, having lived happy lives, when their time comes they accept the dictum of the ancient Epicurean Lucretius that they need to give way to the next generation;

they are grateful to have been alive. Let's say that each of the million people in this world experiences over the course of their life one thousand units of happiness over pain.

Now imagine another world, very different from this one. This world has a billion people in it, but they are all struggling. Life isn't easy for these folks. There isn't enough money for adequate education, and as a result, their technology is underdeveloped. Their land yields just enough for them to eat, so mostly they get by on subsistence levels of nutrition. As a result of scarcity, there are often conflicts among the inhabitants of this world, and those conflicts in turn prevent the kind of cooperation that might lead to social improvement. If you asked these people whether their lives were worth it, they would say yes, but with much less enthusiasm than the folks who live in the other world. Otherwise put, their lives have a balance of happiness over pain—and they recognize that—but that balance does not tip the scales very far in the direction of happiness. Let's say, then, for each of the folks in this world, their lives contain five units of happiness over pain.

We would probably all agree that the first world is better than the second one. There are fewer people in it experiencing happiness—a thousandth, to be exact—but their life experiences are so much better that it more than makes up for the bits of happiness experienced by the greater number of people in the second world. (If the difference doesn't seem enough to you, imagine the second world is even worse, where there is barely any happiness over pain, say two units for each.) However, you've probably already noticed—at least if you don't avoid math as much as I do—that the second world contains more overall happiness than the first one. The first world has a billion units of happiness (a million times a thousand), while the second world has five billion units of happiness (a billion times five).

In short, more happiness does not necessarily make a world better. A worse world might contain more happiness than a better one, depending on how that happiness is distributed.

This argument comes from the work of the influential philosopher Derek Parfit, who gave it the apt name of the Repugnant Conclusion (and who, by the way, thought that extinction would probably be a terrible thing). Although adding happiness to a world does, all things equal, make it a better world, things are rarely equal. And so we can't rest with the conclusion that a better world just is one with more happiness. Otherwise put, one world might have more happiness than another one and yet still not be better. What makes a better world isn't just the aggregate amount of happiness, but the way that happiness is distributed.

How about this, though, as a way around the problem? Maybe a better world isn't one with more aggregate happiness, but instead one with a greater average of happiness? The people in the first world have a much greater average happiness than those in the second one (one thousand to five). So perhaps it's not the amount of happiness that counts but the average of happiness.

Parfit has a response to this as well. To see it, again imagine two worlds, the first of which is like the world imagined a moment ago of a million inhabitants, each of which has a thousand units of happiness over unhappiness. Contrast this with a different world. In this world, there are a million and two inhabitants. Each of the first million inhabitants has eleven hundred units of happiness, but the other two are suffering greatly. Their lives are barely worth living. They experience a half unit of happiness. The mean average happiness of the second world is just under eleven hundred units (1099.998). (If you're looking for a different average, the median would be eleven hundred units, as would the mode.) So this world has a greater average happiness than the first world. But would we really think of it as a better one? We've added just 10 percent more happiness to an already flourishing population, say by making more sporting events available or having even better restaurants or television shows or sunnier weather. But is it worth the suffering of the other two people? Hardly. Because of the way averages work, it is entirely possible to have a world with greater average happiness that, because of the suffering of those at the bottom, would be a worse world than one with a lower average happiness.

What is the upshot of this? The general lesson is that we can't automatically assume that a world with more happiness or even greater average happiness is better than a world with lower aggregate or average happiness. This doesn't mean that adding happiness to the world doesn't make it better. We have already seen that it does. What matters is not just whether or not there is more happiness, but how the happiness is apportioned. More happiness distributed more equitably is a good thing; otherwise, maybe not.

To bring all this back to the question of human extinction, we have at least one reason for there to be humans in the future. We start by assuming, against Benatar, that most humans have lives with more happiness than suffering. Then we add the idea that adding happiness would make the world better. But we recognize, with Parfit, that even if adding happiness makes the world better, a world with more happiness isn't necessarily better than a world with less. Ultimately, what matters is not *only* the amount of happiness, but also how it's spread. So it would be better to add more human beings to the world—because it would add more happiness—but not at the expense of well-distributed happiness. Otherwise put, there is a reason to continue our species, but within certain parameters.

How to achieve optimal levels of happiness would, we can see, be complicated. Overpopulating the planet would lower people's happiness by straining resources, while underpopulating it might bring less happiness than would otherwise be available. In addition, as we will see in the following chapter, we have to take into account the suffering of other creatures that the existence of humans brings. But if we accept that happiness adds something good to the world, then we can come to three tentative conclusions: a) human existence generally adds to the happiness of the world, b) that doesn't mean that adding more humans will necessarily add more happiness, and c) it matters how that happiness is distributed. The first conclusion is key in justifying our continued existence, but the second and third qualify it in important ways.

Human Contributions: Another Perspective

So far we have been considering the value of continuing human existence from the standpoint of the utilitarians. That is, we have looked at how humans make the world better by adding happiness to it. But as we said, utilitarianism must only be part of our framework. There are other angles from which we can consider our contributions, angles that generally fall under the moral view known in philosophy as deontology.

Deontology is not concerned with outcomes or results. For many traditional deontologists, what matters morally are the means or intentions. In their view, it is not the consequences of an action that count; it is the way that act came about.

More recently, much of the focus of deontological thought is on rights and duties; that is, what is owed to people even when it doesn't produce the best results. To give an overly simple example, a utilitarian might endorse sacrificing one innocent person to save two or three other innocent people, since the consequences of that would be better. The deontologist would almost never allow that, because sacrificing the innocent is unacceptable, even when the consequences are better. The sacrifice would violate the right of the individual to their life.*

------

* This example seems to show the utilitarian in a bad light. Sophisticated utilitarians have a way around this, and might also counter with the challenge of whether it's acceptable to sacrifice one innocent person to save a whole city of innocent people—assuming one could find such a city.

The most famous deontologist in the history of philosophy was the eighteenth-century thinker Immanuel Kant. If you've heard of the term "categorical imperative," it comes from Kant. He believed that it wasn't the consequences of an act that mattered morally but rather its intention. And he thought that we could derive good moral intentions through pure reason, without any reference to our emotions or the effects of our action on the world. Fortunately for us, we don't need to go into the details of his moral theory but can skip right to his moral view of human beings, which, it turns out, is an attractive one, both for thinking about ourselves and for giving a sense of why we should continue our species rather than go extinct.

In Kant's view, human beings don't have a value in the sense of economic value. They can't be weighed on any kind of scale. That's why, for instance, you can't sacrifice a human life to save two or three others. (You might ask here whether in saving that one life you're actually sacrificing the others. The basic deontological reply here is that there's a difference between taking lives and failing to save them, where taking them is morally worse.) Kant underlined this idea about human beings by saying that instead of having a value, humans have *dignity*. This dignity cannot be calculated. It's not even infinite, since that would still be on a numerical scale. It's simply beyond measure.

If we take Kant's deontological view, is there a reason it could provide, beyond the utilitarian view of adding happiness to the world, for continuing our existence? The answer turns out to be yes, but it's going to be pretty thin pickings.

Basically, Kant thinks that having reason in the world is a good thing, but that doesn't mean that there should be more of it, or even that there have to be human beings in order to have reason.

To see this, let's start with dignity.

Dignity isn't a value that can or cannot be added to the world. It's immeasurable. In that way, it isn't like happiness. We can say, for instance, that somebody we know is happier than they used to be, but we can't say that they have more dignity than they used to, at least not in the way Kant means it. Dignity, we might say, is not so much a particular quality that a person has or a state of their being like happiness. Instead, it is more like an imperative to others about how a person should be treated. To say that someone has dignity in Kant's sense is to say that they must be respected for themselves rather than just being useful for our own purposes. Kant himself captures this idea in what's called the Second Formulation of his categorical imperative: Treat people always as an end and not merely as a means. The idea is that we can't just take people as tools or objects that we can manipulate as we like. We must recognize that they have lives of their own that we need to respect; we can't reduce their lives to whatever we happen to want from them. Having dignity is like having a kind of moral shield; it protects us against being used just any old way by others.

Why does Kant think that human beings have dignity, though? What is it about us that offers us this moral protection? Maybe, if we dig a little deeper, we might find something that will justify a future for our species. For Kant, the characteristic that humans have that confers our dignity upon us is reason. It's our ability to reason that places us in the realm of moral concern, and in particular our ability to engage in moral reason, to understand the right way to act. And reason, he thought—at least the kind of reason that allows us to be moral—was something that (as far as we know) only human beings possessed. So only human beings have dignity.

But then, isn't the ability to reason morally a good thing to have in the world? Yup. Kant even says so. At the beginning of the first chapter of his book *Groundwork of the Metaphysics of Morals* (a book that's as easy to read as the title would lead you to believe), he says, "There is nothing it is possible to think of anywhere in the world, or indeed anything at all outside it, that can be held to be good without limitation, excepting only a good will." And what is a good will? A will that can act with moral reason. So if it's good that there is good will in the world, and if humans are the only creatures capable of good will, then isn't it good that we stick around?

Here's the thing, though—three things, actually. First, what's good to have in the world is not humans per se, but good will, moral reason. If other things had moral reason, there wouldn't need to be human beings. And, in the age of artificial intelligence, it surely seems possible that there could be other beings with moral reason. They may have a way to go, but they're likely to get there soon enough. (Kant himself, strange to say, was open to the possibility that there could be other beings with reason. Although he didn't

think about AI, of course, he always said that humans were
the only creatures *we're aware of* that have reason.)

Second, what's good is not simply the capacity for moral
reason but real, actual good will. So if human beings all
decided to act without any good will, it's not clear that
Kant would find a place for us.

Finally, remember that dignity and reason don't come in
quantities. There isn't more or less dignity or reason. So as
long as there is reason—moral reason—somewhere in the
world, there is some goodness "without limitation." One
family of humans that could keep propagating its numbers
would do.

So does this mean that Kant gives us *no* reason to continue
the species? It doesn't. He does give us some reason, but, as
I said before, it's pretty thin pickings. Can we do any better?

I think we can. Let's look at two projects that carry on
the spirit of Kant's ideas. Both of them, in their different
ways, will give us reasons to continue the species. It will
take a bit of sorting out, but hey, we're trying to justify
our continued existence here. It isn't like we're asking
whether coffee ice cream is better than mint chocolate chip.
(For the record, coffee is better. But if you think what's coming is at all challenging, you should hear my defense of coffee ice cream.)

An article several years back by the philosopher Sarah
Buss and a recent book by Nandi Theunissen, both entitled
"The Value of Humanity," have argued that we can think of
human beings as having a value that is a shade different from
dignity but still pretty compelling. The term "value" as they

use it isn't economic value but instead a non-quantifiable moral value, sort of like Kant's concept of dignity.

Buss's and Theunissen's views are different, but point in a similar direction. In order to understand them, we'll need get hold of a couple of technical terms in philosophy. In particular, we need to understand the difference between *instrumental* and *non-instrumental* value and the difference between *good* and *good-for*.

Let's tackle them one at a time. Something that only has *instrumental* value has value only inasmuch as it gets you to something else worth having. The classic example is money. Money has no particular value in itself. Its only value lies in the fact that it allows you to get stuff you want to have. Of course, some people treat money as though it were valuable in itself, but that is to mistake the point of money. Money is purely a means; it isn't a goal in itself. By contrast, a *non-instrumental* good doesn't have value solely in getting you to another good. It has value either in itself or in what it does, but isn't, we might say, a station on the way to some other separate good. Remember Kant's Second Formulation of the categorical imperative: Treat people as an end and not solely as a means? (Of course you do.) For Kant, then, people are non-instrumentally good.

The difference between *good* and *good-for* seems at first glance to be similar. "Good-for" is a strange locution, isn't it? To say something is good-for means that it is good for something else. A chair, for instance, is good for sitting on; caffeine is good for energy; my copy of *The Oxford English Dictionary* is good for weight lifting. At first glance, good-for looks like instrumental value while good looks like non-instrumental value. But there is an important difference between these two, which leads to a central debate in moral philosophy. It's in the contrast between good and good-for that we can see it.

There are those philosophers who think there is such a thing as goodness in itself, or Good, full stop. Meaning, they believe that there is good-in-itself beyond any good that can be provided to others. Kant, for instance, thought this about a good will. By contrast, other philosophers, Nandi Theunissen among them, think that to be good must be to be good for something or someone. For her and others in her camp, there is no such thing as just plain Good or good-in-itself, only good-for.

Let's look at a couple of examples. Everyone knows someone they consider to be a morally good person. They're kind, thoughtful, and sensitive to the needs of others. When you call them for help, they're happy to be there for you. They don't forget people's birthdays, and if they know that someone is depressed, they'll check in on them in case there's something they can do. People like this are often models for how we would like to be. They are examples of being good-for. The goodness we're describing here is goodness for others. This doesn't mean they aren't good in themselves; that's a different issue. What I've described here are ways that these people are good-for.

Then there are people we might consider good aside from their impact on other people. They are, we might say, models of what a human being should be. They're friendly, capable, disciplined, and sensitive. (A more traditional but now controversial view might add intelligent, athletic, and good-looking.) We might see them as exemplars of human beings. Even if they never actually have a chance to help anyone or make the world a better place, we would look at them and say that they are good—good-in-themselves. We can assume that if they had a chance to help others, they would. But imagine that, for whatever reason, they don't. We might still look at them as model examples of human beings. They're just good, or Good, depending on your preference for capital letters.

I'm not saying you have to see anyone in this light. (As we'll see, Theunissen doesn't.) The idea is that if we do think of certain people as good-in-themselves, this is how they might appear.

Now we can bring in our ideas of instrumental and intrinsic value as well as good and good-for in order to see how we have reason to continue to exist. Let's look at Sarah Buss's view first, and then turn to Nandi Theunissen's.

Sarah Buss argues that we human beings are valuable, but our value is *only* instrumental. Our value lies in our contribution to something else. However, she thinks, we have an instrumental value that nevertheless justifies treating us as ends-in-ourselves. It sounds like trying to have it both ways, but stay with me. What is this instrumental value Buss thinks we have? It lies in two areas of human existence: our sentience and our rationality.

Human sentience, because of its particular qualities, allows us to appreciate things that are good in themselves but that would otherwise go unappreciated. Take art, for instance. A beautiful painting, according to Buss, has value beyond any experience it might offer to us; however, without human sentience, its beauty would go unappreciated. In order to be appreciated in the way it deserves, she argues, there must exist beings that are capable of undergoing the kind of sentient experience that would allow for this appreciation—beings that can be moved by the beauty of the painting. Non-human animals, as far as we know, can't do that; they don't have the right kind of sensibility. Only human beings are capable of appreciating a beautiful painting, or a profound novel, or a groundbreaking scientific discovery. We are the only living creatures that can have the experiences they offer elicited in us. Therefore, Buss says, human beings should be valued and treated with respect—think Kant's concept of dignity here. That is, we should be treated as ends and not merely as means, because, well, we're the only means we know of to appreciate things that are good-in-themselves.

The place of reason as an instrumental basis of respect is more complicated in Buss's view, but the general idea is that reason, in addition to allowing us to create the kinds of art and science that beg for appreciation, can offer a way to truth. Because of this, we should respect not only our reason but also the reason of other beings that are capable of the discovery of truth. The value of reason here is instrumental, because what we're asked to respect is not the reason of others in itself, as Kant does when he says that having reason confers dignity. Instead, it is that reason is an instrument that can get us toward creation and discovery. If, as many of us think, creation and discovery are good things, then having reason—which allows us to do that—would allow reason to help justify our continuing to be here.

If this is right, then it offers an important consideration in keeping our species going. If we're the only beings that can appreciate art and science and find a way to recognize truth, then it would be a real loss if we went extinct. There wouldn't be anybody left to treasure these things that deserve to be treasured. And that would be a shame.

Like Sarah Buss, Nandi Theunissen also turns away from the idea of defending the value of humans as good-in-themselves. What offers us value is what we are good-for. However, Theunissen does not embrace Buss's view, in part because she is a bit leery of thinking that the value of human sentience lies in its capacity to appreciate something that is good in itself. Buss's view requires us to think of art and truth as good-in-themselves.

But suppose we don't. Buss's view is, after all, a contentious one. The question of whether art is good-in-itself or only good inasmuch as it offers particular experiences to those who can appreciate it is a vexed one in the philosophy of art. Some philosophers, like Buss, like to attribute value to art, as well as to other creations, independent of human engagement with them. A beautiful painting or novel or piece of music, in her view, would be valuable whether or not there were human beings around to appreciate them. What humans offer, Buss would say, is the capacity for the appreciation that these creations deserve because they are valuable in themselves.

Theunissen sees things the other way around. What makes art valuable is not any intrinsic quality it may have, but instead its ability to elicit certain sensibilities in us. We're the source of the value of art rather than art itself.

But if we're the source of such value, what makes us valuable? For Theunissen, our value isn't instrumental, but on the other hand it isn't that we're good-in-ourselves. Instead, our value, although not instrumental, is *relational*. That is, we are valuable in relation to something; what makes us valuable is our relation to that something. So here's the puzzle: How can our value be in relation to something without being instrumental? Isn't instrumental value just value in relation to something else?

Theunissen's thought is that our value is relational, but not relational to something else. It is in our relationship *to ourselves* that we are valuable. To put it in terms we've been using, our goodness lies in our being able to be good-for, but not good-for something else. We aren't, as Buss thinks, good-for art or truth. Instead, we're good-for ourselves. How can this be? Well, the broad idea is that humans can be valuable to ourselves because we can conceive and seek to construct a good life for ourselves.

Let's look at that a little more closely. Unlike other animals, humans can step back and consider ourselves and our lives. We can reflect on the question of what kind of life is worth our living, and then go on to try living it. I can ask myself what would be a worthwhile life for me, think about how I might enact that life in the future, and seek to create it for myself. Among living creatures, so far as we know, only we humans can do that.

Like Buss, Theunissen gives a central role to reason. We have to be able to think about who we are and what we're doing and believing and feeling in order to conceive a good life for us. But unlike Buss, Theunissen thinks that this value lies in our ability to consider and create a good life for ourselves, not in its service of something else. There isn't some other good that creating a good life is supposed to lead us toward. The point of thinking about and creating a good life is, well, to create a good life. That's it. And so, she says, our value is in relation (to ourselves) and not instrumental (for the sake of something else).

The idea of a good being relational and non-instrumental at the same time may strike us as strange or counterintuitive. Think of this, though. Contrast a hammer's relation to furniture with our relationship to our lives. A hammer is instrumentally valuable because it helps us build a piece of furniture. It is the furniture as a distinct product that gives the hammer its value. Otherwise the hammer wouldn't have any value at all. The hammer, then, is both relational and instrumental: relational to the furniture and instrumental to building it.

But my relation to my life isn't like that. It isn't instrumental. In building my life, I'm not trying to make something else better or more interesting or more balanced or whatever. I'm trying to make *my life* better or more interesting or more balanced or whatever. I'm building my own life, not something or someone else. So I'm in relationship—to my life—but not as an instrument to make something else better or more interesting or . . . Well, you get the idea.

Both Buss and Theunissen in their different ways offer us paths to thinking about why it might be valuable to continue our species. Not that they're trying to do that. Neither of these philosophers is seeking to offer a reason for continuing humanity into the future. Their concerns lie not with who might come after us, but with us here and now and as we are.

However, there is something common to both of their views that can offer a path to justifying future human existence—something that lies in the way they think of the human ability to have sophisticated relationships to a variety of things. If we put their views into a common form, we can see that there is a special ability that humans have that, so far as we can tell, lies beyond what other animals are capable of. We might characterize that ability in a sort of shorthand as the capacity to experience, create, and engage with beauty, truth, and a good life. There is more, to be sure, but if we put Buss's ideas of sentience and rationality together with Theunissen's idea of people's relationship to themselves through conceiving and seeking to enact a good life, we get something like this: Humans have a capacity that belongs to no other animal—or, at the very least, to no other animal to anywhere near the degree that humans have it—to have certain valuable relationships, relationships to beauty, truth, and a good life.

(As a side note, we can see here how Buss and Theunissen are thinking in the philosophical tradition that Kant opened up but adding something richer as well. Reason plays an important role in their views; but it's not reason alone that confers value on humanity. Rather, it is particular engagements of reason—as well as our particular sentience—in the world that form the basis for respecting humans.)

If this is right, then we have, independent of any happiness we can bring into the world—whether through ourselves or others—another reason for continuing our species. Were humans to cease to exist, there would no longer be such experiences. And these experiences would be much more difficult to replicate in an artificial intelligence program. That, to my mind, would be a tragic loss. The world would be impoverished in an important way if there were no longer beings who could experience beauty, truth, and the possibility of a good life.

To see why, we can engage in a similar thought experiment to the ones we did earlier with happiness. This time, picture a world in which humans were happy, enjoying their food and sleep and one another—in much the same way other animals do—but did not have any experiences of beauty or truth. They could not see the beauty in various sports, say a graceful move in basketball or a swimmer that glides effortlessly through the water. Their experiences of novels would be more or less like our experiences of journalism; they would learn facts about fictional beings without any type of empathy toward them or resonance with their own experience. An insight revealed by science would be just a fact without any sense of the world that is being enlightened by that insight.

In fact, we can go further. There would likely be no sports or novels or science, which require an appreciation of the point of these activities in order for anyone to engage in them in the first place. And along with that, there would be no vision of a good life to be achieved. To use Mill's term, these humans would have no access to what he called the higher pleasures.

What we're describing here is, to a great extent, the lives of most non-human animals. Because of the limitations of their reason and, relatedly, their emotional range, they cannot create or appreciate many of the activities and products that humans can. They move from meal to meal, protecting themselves and their offspring from predators, relating to one another, and generally carving out their ecological niche. It might be strange to describe them as happy—or at least happy at times—but I suspect that many animals have a sense of joy, a sense that is evidenced in the various forms of play that animals with more advanced cognition engage in. We've all seen those nature documentaries in which dogs or bears or chimpanzees or pigs, especially young ones, tease and paw and jump on one another. And I suspect that we've all been caught up in the joyous emotion of watching them go at one another. If there is such a thing as animal happiness, that, to my mind, has to be an example of it.

But let's imagine that that's all, that there is nothing more to the creatures of the world, including humans, than that: food, sleep, sex, relationships, basic things like that. Would that not be a loss? Wouldn't the world be impoverished without the experiences of creating and appreciating beauty, truth, and the possibilities of a good life? It seems to me, and I don't think I'm alone in this, that if these experiences came to an end, it would be a tragedy. The world would become a bit hollowed out; it would lose some of its richness.

As with happiness, I don't have a particular argument to show that anyone must believe that this would be a loss. Instead, I can only draw the picture and ask whether you see what I see. It's entirely open for someone, I suppose someone like Benatar, to feel unmoved—or at least largely unmoved—by the experiences of beauty, truth, and the good life. And in that case, there might be nothing on the side of the scale that weighs in favor of continued human existence. However, I think the prospect of a world bereft of these experiences would seem for most of us like a terrible loss.

At this point you may recall the earlier discussion of meaningfulness and narrative values, the idea that a life can be meaningful beyond being just happy, because of certain themes it expresses, like spontaneity or intensity or adventurousness. What might be the relation between meaningfulness and the experiences we're considering here? After all, they both involve ways of being engaged with the world. Narrative values are themes of a life that moves through the world in certain ways or with a certain style. The experiences of beauty, truth, and the good life are also ways of being engaged with the world, though often more limited in temporal scope. We appreciate a piece of music or create a mathematical truth or reflect on how our lives should go.

At this point, you may suspect—you might even say with good reason!—that I have left something important out of this discussion of important human experiences: love. I'm not trying to be cold-hearted. No doubt love is indeed among the most important relationship experiences that we have in our lives. The reason I have left it out so far is that I've been focusing on experiences that are particularly human ones. And while it's an arguable point, the experience of love does not, to my mind, belong solely to human beings. And so I am leaving it for the following chapter, where we can contrast human love and the love between various non-human animals, love that is often stifled through human activity.

Extinction as a Loss for Those of Us Who Already Exist

So far, we have looked at two ways in which the continued existence of humanity can be justified: through the addition of happiness and through the existence of experiences of beauty, truth, and the good life. There is a third justification as well, one that has been brought to attention recently by the philosopher Samuel Scheffler. In a piece in the *New York Times* followed up by two books, *Death and the Afterlife* and the more technical *Why Worry About Future Generations?*, Scheffler offers a reason for continuing our species that is grounded in humanity itself rather than in what we might contribute to the world. His idea is that in order for the lives of currently existing people to be fully meaningful, we must believe that humanity will continue. (Readers of a certain generation—mine—might recall here Jonathan Schell's 1982 blockbuster, *The Fate of the Earth*, which scared the daylights out of us by picturing the end of human life after a nuclear holocaust.)

It's not, for Scheffler, simply that we must *want* humanity to continue in the form of our kids. Of course those of us who have or know children want that, and many people who don't yet have kids will want humanity to continue through kids they will conceive. (Although, as we know, in the current generation of young adults there is deep ambivalence about bringing kids into a world where climate disaster is beginning to take hold.) But part of what lends our lives a sense of significance, Scheffler argues, is the future existence of people to whom we will have no relation and of whom we will have no knowledge, many of whom will come to exist after we die.

To see what he means, let's look at some examples. An obvious although unrepresentative one would be the researcher who seeks a cure for cancer. Right now there are a number of researchers doing this. Their assumption is that they may not find the cure in their lifetimes, but they'll pass what they've learned on to the next generation of researchers in the hope that eventually there will be a cure. Suppose though, that, in a *Children of Men* scenario, there will be no next generation. (Scheffler himself refers to *Children of Men*.)

Suppose that when these researchers die, so will their research. Unless they're confident that they can come up with a cure during their lifetimes, it's not clear that what they're doing has any point.

Cancer researchers are a small minority of humanity. However, if we widen the lens we can see that the significance of the lives of many if not most of us is dependent to one extent or another on the existence of future generations of people we will never meet. As a first step, think of writers, engineers, entrepreneurs who create businesses, construction workers who build homes, teachers who seek to pass on the wisdom of historians or playwrights or psychologists or carpenters. Think of anyone who belongs to a tradition that they find important or worthwhile enough not only to participate in but to pass along to others or even just think is worth passing along to others. This can be as far-flung as being a sports fan or a member of a Rotary Club or someone who plants trees for others to enjoy when those trees mature. If there were no future generations to follow them, some of the point of their lives would surely bleed away. Not all of it, to be sure, but often not just a little bit, either.

We might resist this idea by pointing out that we enjoy many of these activities in the moment, so it doesn't require future generations to make them meaningful to us. This would certainly be the perspective of a Buddhist or a Stoic, for instance. I agree that we all seek an enjoyment of the moment to some degree or another. And for sure it's not entirely the continued existence of these activities that gives them their point. But consider this. There are people who build small businesses—grocery stores or restaurants or pharmacies—that may have to close them at some point for one reason or another. Maybe, after years, the market changes or the neighborhood becomes too pricey to operate in. Or maybe when the owner gets too old to keep up the work, there is nobody to sell the business to. Or maybe the kids just want their own lives and aren't interested in continuing the operation. Even where it's been meaningful to create and run the business for so many years—important in the moments of running it—the anticipation of its closure is often fraught with sorrow and even regret. So it isn't just the moments themselves that matter to us most of the time—it's also the future that those moments are contributing to.

We can follow Scheffler's idea further still. Wouldn't the prospect of the end of humanity, even if the lives of the current generation were not to be cut short, be a prospect filled with sadness or despair? This book, the one you're reading now, is a difficult one to write, and no doubt is difficult for many of you to read. (Emotionally, I mean. Hopefully not literally. Philosophy!) This is because the possibility of the end of human existence is a depressing one to contemplate. Of course, we all know that eventually humanity will have to end, if for no other reason than that the gradual expansion of the sun will swallow up the planet. But somehow putting it that way seems to most of us to be a very distant prospect. If we bring that prospect closer and ask about the end of humanity coinciding with the end of our lives, this is a much more dismal scenario to reflect upon.

Scheffler argues that just as the existence and health of future generations depends on us and what we do, important aspects of what makes our lives worthwhile depends on those future generations—and in particular on their coming to exist. The end of humanity not only deprives future generations of the joys of existence (although, as we have seen, nobody in particular is deprived since there isn't yet anybody in particular among those who haven't been born); it also deprives us of important dimensions of what makes our lives significant to us.

A Return to Who's Asking, and a Smaller Population

We have seen, then, three reasons for continuing humanity into the future. First, it would add happiness to the world. Second, it would continue the existence of important experiences that only human beings are capable of having (or having to a degree of richness) with the world. Finally, it would help sustain the sense of significance of people who currently exist.

We are about to look at some downsides of our continued existence. Before we do, though, there are two questions left over to confront. First, returning to a question that we initially posed near the end of the previous chapter, doesn't all this presuppose a human viewpoint? If there were no humans, would any of this really matter? Second, wouldn't all these reasons to keep making humans be the same if the human population were much smaller than it is now, so do we really need to consider complete extinction? Wouldn't a million people as opposed to the eight billion we have now be sufficient for fulfilling all three considerations in favor of humanity?

Great questions, these. On the first question, here's the challenge: The idea of adding happiness to the world as a contribution to its betterment is an idea that only a human can have. Other animals don't think about these things. Suppose, then, that humans no longer existed. For whom would less happiness be a deprivation? Not for any of the creatures who would still exist. So in what sense would it be a loss? Similarly, if there were no creation or appreciation of art or sports or science, to whom would it matter? Other animals don't care about these things, as far as we can tell. Only human beings do, and we're asking the question on this side of human extinction. If we no longer existed, there would be nobody who would miss these experiences.

If we go back to Scheffler for a moment, we can see why all this should matter to us now, on this side of extinction. Knowing that there would be nobody to follow us is an impoverishment of our lives, the lives of currently existing people. It is, of course, a human worry, and if there were no longer any humans, there would be nobody to be concerned with this. But the effect on us of an imminent extinction would be an effect on us now, on we who do exist, sapping our lives of some of the significance they might otherwise have. We who are here, if we think about it, *are* concerned. We—okay, most of us who aren't in Benatar's camp—don't want there to be a world in which there isn't anybody to have these experiences.

It is true, of course, that if human beings no longer existed, there would be nobody to be concerned with our continued happiness and so on. And it's also true—and part of the point—that these concerns come from a human perspective. However, in asking about the character of a future world both with and without us, we are asking it from the only standpoint from which it can be asked: a human standpoint. Our standpoint. We are evaluating the prospect of our continued existence from the perspective we occupy, which is the only one available to us. We look upon the world, consider what it would be like if we continue to exist and compare that with what it would be like if we didn't continue to exist, and ask about the good and bad aspects of each of these scenarios. How else could an evaluation like that happen except through human inquiry?

This does not mean that the "human perspective" or the "us" I'm referring to involves a single agreed-upon viewpoint. As we've already seen, there are those, like Benatar, who could take a human perspective and not be persuaded by all the good stuff I'm associating with continued human existence. The human perspective is not a single unified perspective; rather, it's the ability to put the issue up for discussion. What would go missing without our perspective is not just a future loss that wouldn't matter to those creatures who continue to exist. It is also the ability to raise the question of what kind of loss that might be. Only currently existing humans can ask that question, even if it turns out that the answer is that it would not be much of a loss at all, or—more disturbing to contemplate—a benefit.

In posing the question to ourselves, are we answering it—or disagreeing about how to answer it—in part on behalf of the interests of non-human animals who will or will not continue to share the world with us? Yes, we are. We have nowhere else to turn for an answer. The only alternative is not to ask the question at all, and that doesn't seem to me to be a philosophical improvement over asking it from our standpoint.

Let's turn, then, to the second question. Would the addition of happiness and the experience of beauty, truth, and the good life and so on be the same in a much smaller population, one less likely to cause all the problems we'll see in the following chapter? Would anything of significance be forfeited if there were a lot fewer of us around than there are now? We will return to the impact of a smaller human population a little farther down the road, but for the moment we can ask about its relevance for the reasons we have seen for continuing our existence.

The first reason—adding more happiness—is the most complicated one from this perspective. In following the arguments of Derek Parfit, we saw that more happiness is not necessarily better—it depends on how that happiness is spread around. The Repugnant Conclusion—the idea that there can be a much larger population with very little individual happiness that would have more aggregate happiness

than a smaller population with more individual happiness—
shows that adding happiness through adding human beings
would not always result in an improved world, even if each
human being brought along some happiness with them.
This, by itself, doesn't answer the question of whether it
would be better for there to be a much smaller human population. The calculations here would be difficult. We would
have to figure out how to balance the individual happiness
of the people involved with the aggregate happiness of the
total population. The most we can say is that having more
as opposed to fewer humans, although it might increase aggregate or even average happiness, cannot by itself answer
the question of how many humans would be optimal. It
would depend on issues like the availability of resources and
the distribution of goods.

How about the other two benefits of our continued existence: the creation, discovery, and appreciation of beauty,
truth, and a good life as well as Scheffler's concern? Regarding the first, it seems that a smaller human population
would do just as well as a larger one. What is at stake is a
diversity of creations and forms of appreciation. There need
to be enough humans to support that diversity, but once
that level is reached it doesn't strike me as terribly important that there be more such experiences. Having people
who paint and write novels and engage in science and sports
and other types of human creation, both as participants and
as appreciative audiences, is an addition to the world. But at
a certain point the quantity of these experiences does not
seem to matter. It's the existence of these activities rather

than their proliferation that adds a dimension to the world. A much smaller population could accomplish just as much good in this realm as a much larger one.

Scheffler's concern that the meaning of our lives is bound up with the existence of future generations could also be met with a much smaller population. His point is that there needs to be a next generation to carry on the activities, traditions, and projects of the current generation. It needs to be large enough to be able to carry on those things, but beyond that, size doesn't matter. The important point for him is continuity, and so, once again, a much smaller human population will do just as well as a larger one.

Of course, if history is any guide, smaller human populations tend to turn into larger ones, and those larger ones are creating some of the problems that have motivated the reflections in this book. That's a problem. To see why, it's time to take a deep breath and look at the bad news. It isn't going to be pretty, but looking away is no solution. Join me, then, on the next step of our journey.

THREE

The Other Side
of the Ledger

HERE IS A DESCRIPTION OF the life of dairy cows on a factory farm:

> The U.S. is home to more than 9 million dairy cows. Many of these intelligent, sensitive individuals face intense confinement in unsanitary conditions and are treated like milk-producing machines. Then, after a life of suffering to produce milk, they are sent to slaughter the minute they become unprofitable. . . .
>
> Cows farmed for dairy are forcibly impregnated and then have their young taken from them soon after birth, so that their milk, which would naturally be suckled by a calf, can be sold for human consumption. This process, which is emotionally traumatizing for the mother cow and her baby, is repeated in a continuous cycle . . .
>
> Intensively raised dairy cows have been selectively bred

over time to produce unnaturally high quantities of milk. The amount of milk produced by a single cow has doubled in the past 40 years, which puts an immense strain on her body. To further increase milk yield, they are sometimes injected with bovine somatotropin, a growth hormone that has been linked to increased risk of mastitis, infertility, and lameness.

Rather than being allowed to graze on grass and other vegetation as they would naturally, dairy cows in factory farms are fed a diet high in processed cereal grains such as corn and wheat. These grains are cheap to buy and maximize the cows' milk yield but, because they are high in starch and low in fiber, they can cause digestive illness in cows.

Despite having a natural lifespan of around 20 years, mother cows used in the dairy industry are typically killed at between 4.5 and 6 years of age. At this point, their bodies are no longer able to produce enough milk to make it profitable to keep them alive. . . .

Cows who are too sick or injured to even move, labeled "downers," are killed on-farm. . . . Others are sent to slaughterhouses and enter the human food chain as cheap, processed meat products such as ground beef. After a long journey on a filthy, overcrowded truck, without food and water, these cows are lined up, restrained, stunned, and have their throats slit. Pre-slaughter stunning is supposed to render animals unconscious and unable to feel pain, but it does not always work and animals can suffer a slow, painful death.

Over 70 percent of cows are raised on factory farms, either as dairy cows or beef cows. That amounts to roughly nine million dairy cows and thirty million beef cows that live on factory farms.

And here is a description of the life of pigs on a factory farm:

In pigs, the natural weaning process takes two to three months, but on factory farms piglets are taken away from their mothers after just three to four weeks. They are then crowded into metal-barred and concrete-floored pens in giant warehouses where they will live until they are separated to be raised for breeding or meat. More than one million pigs die annually just during transport to slaughter, and as many as 10 percent of pigs are "downers," animals who are so ill or injured that they are unable to stand and walk on their own.

Factory farmed male piglets are frequently castrated without anesthesia or pain relief. . . .

In addition to overcrowded housing, pigs also endure extreme crowding during transportation. This crowding often results in rampant suffering and death, even before they arrive at the slaughterhouse. At the slaughterhouse, pigs are first supposed to be "stunned" and rendered unconscious. . . . However, stunning at slaughterhouses is terribly imprecise. Conscious pigs are often left to hang upside down, kicking and struggling, while a slaughterhouse worker attempts to slice their throats. If the worker is unsuccessful at this first station, the pigs will be carried to the next station on the slaughterhouse assembly line, the scalding tank, and boiled alive fully conscious.

Roughly 105 million pigs, 97 percent of all pigs raised in the United States, are raised on factory farms.

This is not even the worst of it. Veal cows are raised in small crates that restrict their ability to move so that their flesh remains tender. Foie gras is made by force-feeding ducks and geese. We saw briefly in the first chapter what the lives of chickens on factory farms is like. In all, every year many millions of animals are raised in egregious conditions, live short and miserable lives, and are often killed in painful and even cruel ways.

.   .   .

Why linger over the details of animal suffering on factory farms? In the previous chapter we saw that the continued existence of human beings—that is, us—adds something positive to the world. One aspect of what we add—happiness—is grounded in utilitarianism, the philosophy that counsels us that we should act in such a way as to cause the greatest amount of happiness over unhappiness.

The key here, however, is causing happiness *over unhappiness* or suffering. An act that causes happiness, but at the expense of greater unhappiness, is not a good utilitarian act. If I buy you a nice box of Godiva chocolates with money I have stolen from a food bank that because of my theft has had to leave a family without sufficient food, then I have not done the right thing. Your enjoyment of the chocolate and of the generosity of my giving it to you is outweighed by the suffering of the family without food. If we're going to tally the value of additional human happiness in succeeding generations, we also have to subtract the negative value that human beings create through the suffering we inflict on other sentient beings. And, as we will see, we create a lot of negative value.

Look, we humans like to think of ourselves as morally decent. (Okay, most of us do. A few of us—not naming names but they know who they are!—don't really care.) We are creatures of reason. Unlike a lot of other animals, we basically know right from wrong and we often try our best to do the right thing. To think that our living is causing more suffering than the good we're contributing is emotionally wrenching. And further, to think that it's possible that all of us—the whole lot of human beings—are causing staggering levels of suffering just through our being here is super painful. And yet, here we are. It may be that that's what we're doing. In any event, let's not look away.

Is it certain, though, that all the suffering we're causing outweighs what we bring to the world? In this chapter, we'll try to get a grip on this, if not the total balance of what we contribute as against the suffering we cause, at least a sense of the immensity of that suffering. In doing so, we'll look at three issues in particular: the unhappiness we produce over and against the happiness we would contribute; the misery we create over and against the experiences of truth, beauty, and the good life; and the threat we pose to ecosystems.

Comparing Human and Animal Happiness

Let's look at the United States for a moment. The population of this country is currently a bit over 330 million. If we take the number of farm animals slaughtered each year for consumption, we can begin to get an idea of the suffering inflicted by U.S. animal consumption. Over the past few years, on average roughly 130 million pigs per year are slaughtered in the United States. Add to that 8 billion chickens and 32 million cows. So each American consumes, on average, one third of a pig, twenty-four chickens, and a cow per year. Assuming, again roughly, that a typical American lives around seventy-five years, sixty-five of which are taken up with meat consumption, this is equivalent to nearly 22 pigs, 1,560 chickens, and 65 cows.

This doesn't even include the suffering we inflict on other farm animals, such as ducks, as well as on animals that are used in scientific experimentation, those suffering because of deforestation and the disposing of plastics, and the abuse endured by fellow animals in other ways.

Of course, somebody might say, we don't just cause suffering to animals. Take this person's cat Tabby, for instance. Tabby's a happy cat. He has a great life. He doesn't worry about where his next meal is coming from, has a warm place to sleep in the winter, and a litter box that this person always keeps clean for him. And what's more, this person's friends have cats too—happy cats. There are a lot of happy pets in the world. Don't they count for something? Shouldn't we factor that in? And what's more, the lives of factory-farmed animals must have *some* happiness associated with them. It can't be all suffering. After all, these animals struggle against death right up to their very last moments. Don't they have a modicum of happiness that wouldn't be there if we never brought them into the world?

Let's get clear on a couple of things. First, although we'll be doing some comparisons here, there is no precise mathematical formula that will tell us whether the amount of happiness that humans experience and bring into the world exceeds the amount of suffering and unhappiness we create through our treatment of non-human animals. Calculating the suffering we cause animals and comparing it to the happiness we bring into the world is not, and cannot be, a simple numbers game. One reason for this is that there isn't a single scale on which to measure them.

Why isn't there such a scale? Humans are capable not only of different amounts of happiness but also different types of happiness and unhappiness, some of which aren't available to other animals. This is because our cognitive abilities offer us access to experiences that non-human animals, especially those like pigs, cows, and chickens, cannot have. So in comparing human happiness with the happiness of non-human animals, it's not apples to apples, but apples to oranges, or maybe apples to operas.

It is central to human life that we live toward the future

and in an awareness of the past. We see our lives as trajectories, starting somewhere and passing through various and diverse stages until we reach our end. We think about our future as connected to our past; not only that, we also think about our death and what death signifies for the arc of our lives. All of this means that we undergo expectation and anticipation, regret and remorse, enthusiasm and anxiety, that require a full human consciousness in order to be able to experience.

Now, some might say that other animals can experience these emotions to one degree or another. That may be true. In teaching courses on animals rights, I have learned that other animals have much richer lives than I previously imagined. However, for us human beings the recognition of our lives as coming from a past, extending into a future, and ending in death is centrally organizing for our approach to life. It is who we are in ways that I suspect would be unavailable to animals without a significant capacity for cognitive awareness. And among those animals who will lack that capacity are chickens, cows, and to a lesser extent, pigs.

What we might call the *richness* of human lives, then, offers dimensions of happiness and unhappiness that cannot be placed on the same scale as that of other animals. This, in turn, makes comparisons of our experience of happiness and the suffering we produce elusive at best.

I would argue that the richness of human experience makes humans capable not only of other dimensions of happiness but even of greater degrees of it. This is because, in addition to the happiness that most animals experience—food, sleep, sex, care for their young and their compatriots—humans can experience the joys of art, science, sports, and other activities we canvassed in the previous chapter. To be sure, we also have experiences of suffering that are outside the range of non-human animals. If I injure myself, for instance, I will worry about what this means for my job and future health. But if we hold to the view I proposed in the previous chapter in discussing Benatar's position—that for most of us, our lives are more or less happy and at least worth living—then we can tentatively assume that the happiness we experience through the richness of human life generally outweighs the unhappiness that that richness also brings.

On behalf of human beings—again, that is us—I've been arguing that we can experience dimensions of happiness that are unavailable to other animals and that those dimensions add types of happiness above and beyond what non-human animals experience, although not measurable on the same scale. So in comparing the happiness we contribute to the world against the suffering we cause other animals, we can say that, even without a single scale of measurement, human beings are capable of greater levels of happiness than non-human animals. That's not to say that Bob the depressive is happier than Tabby the cat. Rather, it's to open the possibility that the continued existence of human beings in general might *outweigh* the suffering we cause to the animals around us.

But really, is that true? I can hear Tabby's owner now, telling me that other animals have their own kinds of experiences, unavailable to humans, that might offer their own dimensions of happiness. Dogs might get an extra thrill from a good smell because of their sensitive nasal apparatus. Cats might experience a visual pleasure that is beyond our capacity because of our limited visual capacities. Elephants have particularly good hearing; they might enjoy sounds that we can't even perceive. Perhaps, then, there is no difference between humans and non-humans on a scale of "richness of experience." There are just different, well, richnesses.

There are two problems with this argument. The first is that for humans, our types of richness of experience don't concern the idea of getting more out of certain senses. They are instead experiences of a different kind. Intellectual and artistic engagement are not just about more visual or auditory pleasure; they are different dimensions of happiness, adding different levels of richness to our experience.

Nevertheless, Tabby's owner might reply, can't the amount of, say, auditory pleasure offset the different dimension of artistic pleasure? Or, if not, since artistic pleasure is on a different scale, might it at least make the idea of the greater richness of human experience moot, since the two are incomparable? This is where the second problem for Tabby's owner comes in.

Suppose we were to say that there is no difference between the richness of human experience and that of many other animals. And suppose then that we were put in a position where we had to choose between sacrificing the life of a human and that of a dog. What would be the justification for sacrificing the dog instead of the human? We can't just say that we're saving the human because it's human. That's the question at issue. If we just stop at the idea that we're saving a human simply because it is a human, then we run into the problem of what the philosopher Peter Singer and other animal rights theorists call "speciesism." Speciesism is the privileging of one species over another for arbitrary reasons. If we're going to privilege one species over another in a certain case, we should have a good reason for doing so.

What would be a good reason to save the human and allow the dog to be sacrificed? A standard answer is that a human being would have more to lose than a dog and so we should save the human. But what's the reason for that? Well, humans have the potential for richer experience than dogs, which gives them more to lose. Sometimes people say that humans have a greater cognitive capacity than dogs, but to my mind cognitive capacity is not exactly the point when it comes to what humans lose by being sacrificed. Instead it's the richness of experience that our cognitive capacity allows us to have. Combined with the earlier argument, we seem to have a good reason to say that in general humans have the capacity for richer experiences than non-human animals and therefore the comparison between a human and another animal as far as adding happiness to the world would most often tilt toward the human.

Factory Farming and Animal Suffering

So far we've focused on the complexity of comparing human and non-human animal happiness. There are two important points here. One is that there is no simple mathematical formula for comparing human happiness with the happiness of other animals, in particular the animals to which we cause pain and suffering. The other is that humans are capable of dimensions of happiness that other animals just aren't. Might this second point help establish that human happiness outweighs the suffering we cause?

Nope.

This is because most of us cause or at least participate in causing immense suffering to other animals, particularly but not exclusively those raised on factory farms. As we've seen in regard to factory farming, neglecting for the moment issues like deforestation, disposal of plastic, contribution to the climate crisis, scientific experimentation, and competition for natural resources, an average U.S. life—a single one—costs the suffering of roughly 22 pigs, 1,560 chickens, and 65 cows.

Even though we can't come up with a mathematical comparison, the unavoidable conclusion is that the existence of the average American comes at the expense of extraordinary suffering. Is bringing a human life into the world worth all this suffering? A strict comparison may be impossible, but it is clearly a live question. And it's going to get liver still. (That's "liver" with a long "i.")

But what about Tabby, and Tabby's colleagues, and all those little bits of happiness that factory-farmed animals are capable of? Hey, even without doing a mathematical comparison, it's easy to see that whatever bits of happiness a factory-farmed animal experiences are overwhelmed by the suffering it undergoes. And even if we add the happiness of well-tended pets into the equation (minus the difficult lives of many abandoned and feral animals), I don't see that we subtract much from the unhappiness, indeed the agony, our existence causes to the non-human animal world.

But really, aren't we just talking about the suffering U.S. consumption causes, not human consumption in general? Look back at those numbers. They aren't the numbers of factory-farmed animals slaughtered by human beings; they're the number of factory-farmed animals slaughtered by *Americans*! Is that really fair? Is it fair to condemn humanity on the basis of the suffering caused by one small part of it? Wouldn't things look different if we looked at human consumption in general? Wouldn't they even look different if we focused on subsets of Americans, say vegans or vegetarians?

The answer here is partly yes, but mostly no. Partly yes: We in the United States eat a lot of meat. A whole lot. As a result, compared with other and larger populations in places like India and China, we cause a bunch more suffering to other animals through our consumption of factory-farmed animals. There's a reason McDonald's, Burger King, KFC, Wendy's, Chick-fil-A, and Zaxby's all started in the United States, and it doesn't just have to do with the weather.

But mostly no: As nations become more prosperous, their citizens eat more meat. In China, for instance, meat consumption has been steadily rising since at least the 1990s. (There are even pig-farming skyscrapers being built there.) And in India, a country with very low meat consumption—meat-eating has risen in recent years as a middle class develops in that country. Poultry consumption in India, for instance, has skyrocketed over the past decade. Given that China and India account for nearly three billion of the eight billion people currently on the planet, we can expect that as people become more affluent, meat consumption will increase and with it the egregious practices associated with factory farming.

Now, don't misunderstand me here. I'm not saying that the increase in material affluence of countries like China and India is a bad thing for those who live there. People who are alive deserve to have access to the resources that will allow them to live flourishing lives. In fact, many of us who can afford to—and I include myself in this—do not do enough to ensure that those without adequate resources for living are provided them. This is a matter of justice for those who are currently alive. Just as I argued against mass suicide in the first chapter, so it is clear that those who are alive deserve a chance to flourish.

The question we're interested in instead concerns the bringing of others into existence. If we bring people into the world, we have an obligation to offer them as best we can the possibility of at least a decent life. What the trends in China and India tell us is that as people become more prosperous, their consumption of meat rises, and with it the suffering associated with factory farming. The United States represents an extreme point of this trend, but it is the terminus toward which other countries are moving. As they tend in that direction, the amount of suffering they cause increases. And as the amount of suffering they cause increases, it becomes more difficult to justify our future existence here.

What About the Nice Farms?

Does this mean that we cannot justify the eating of meat at all? Does the fact of meat-eating itself diminish the justification for continued human existence? Not necessarily. There are, for instance, farms that offer alternatives to mass production of meat. The question of eating meat from those farms is morally complicated. On the one hand, it could be argued that well-treated animals on these farms have good lives that they would not otherwise have had if they were not raised for meat. Insofar as that happens, these animals add to the amount of happiness that exists in the world. Moreover, if we compare the lives of animals on well-tended farms with the lives of many animals in the wild, we will likely see that the lives of the former may be much better. We can't directly compare domesticated animals like cows and chickens and pigs with deer or gazelles or beavers. However, we can comfortably say that deer and gazelles and beavers spend a good bit of their conscious lives concerned with the possibility of being eaten, and when they are eaten, it is often in staggeringly painful ways. (More on that in a moment.) By contrast, cows, pigs, and chickens raised in a benevolent way and killed in a humane manner will experience happiness that is unavailable to much prey that lives in the wild.

On the other hand, of course, someone could say that once you've brought an animal into existence, it isn't fair to kill it. Bringing living beings into the world carries with it responsibilities, we might say, at the very least the responsibility not to murder it. So while alternatives to factory farming might add more happy lives to the world, whether it's okay to slaughter them for meat remains an open question.

Human Suffering—An Aside

We're focused here on the suffering that humans inflict upon animals and on asking whether, in the face of that, our continued existence is justified. There are some—maybe more than some—who might ask whether the suffering we visit upon our fellow human beings also raises the question of whether our continued existence is justified. Does the pain we humans have a penchant for causing our fellow humans give us a reason not to continue?

I'm not asking whether we as a species deserve to continue, given the harm we cause one another. Recall from the first chapter that what we deserve is not the issue. Rather, might the suffering we cause one another make it worse in a utilitarian way for the species to continue? Might human-on-human suffering cause more overall misery to humans than happiness? And if so, wouldn't that be a reason to exit the stage?

I argued in the previous chapter against Benatar that for most of us, our lives are worth living. Sure, there is plenty of suffering that we go through, and plenty of difficulty that we cause one another. But in the end, I think, most of us are grateful to have been brought into existence. Will that continue?

I can imagine a situation in which it wouldn't. Suppose the climate crisis were to become so severe that a large segment of the human population was suffering greatly from it. Suppose, for instance, that of the ten billion people that are likely to populate the planet in five or six decades, while seven billion people lived decent lives, three billion were in climate agony. If we're going to be utilitarians about this, let's put some numbers on it. Suppose that each of the seven billion people had ten units of happiness, while each of the other three billion had thirty units of misery. And let's further suppose that in order for those ten billion to have their ten units of happiness, they had to contribute enough to climate devastation that the other three billion would continue their agony.

Overall, there would be more suffering than happiness, twenty billion units to be exact. Well, in that case extinction might, on a utilitarian calculus, be our best option. Even though there would be lots of people with good lives, the overall misery would override the overall happiness.

Could we really imagine this happening? In some ways, that might not be so difficult. Many of us who are better off economically often ignore the hardship of those who pay the costs of our good fortune. We don't think about the lives of delivery people, sanitation workers, food service folks, people who build and maintain our homes and roads, many of whose low pay and difficult working conditions keep our costs down and make our lives easier. Of course, most of these folks have lives worth living. We're imagining things getting worse for them in the future. For example, along with the devastation that our carbon emissions cause non-human animals, there are effects on those who are poor and badly situated. It would not be a stretch to imagine a future where overall suffering is greater than overall happiness: workers outside or in kitchens in extreme heat, poor people without access to water or affordable food, regular flooding of homes that are in low-lying areas. The difference would be that instead of seven billion happy and three billion suffering, it would be the other way around, or worse.

We might then ask why people would allow this, if they would, and whether allowing it would be a further argument for our demise. We could ask this as a question about what we would deserve; that would be a question posed to the three billion (or fewer) happy people. Or we could ask a broader question: Would any of us be untroubled about being in the three billion if we knew, or at least sensed, the suffering that is the basis for our comfort?

This question leads to larger speculations about human nature. Is the callousness of which (some? many?) people seem capable innate, or is it the product of particular cultures or histories? Some would argue that human character is something that can largely be shaped by circumstances— social, political, or cultural encouragement leads us to join the three billion living off the misery of others. For others, there is something inherently unseemly about us, prone to exclude those who are designated as others and even perhaps capable of cruelty toward them. This is a larger debate, one we aren't going to be able to decide here. But it goes to deep questions about who we are, questions that have haunted philosophers—and the rest of us—over the millennia of human existence.

Deforestation

So far, we have kept our focus on one way—although a central one—in which human existence brings suffering into the world. The consumption of factory-farmed animals causes colossal levels of suffering, enough that it is unclear whether our continued existence is justified, however we try to defend ourselves. And factory farming isn't the only way we create suffering for other animals. Let's briefly consider another: deforestation.

In expanding agriculture and grazing land, humanity has deforested large areas of the planet. Moreover, deforestation is accelerating, both through the expansion of the human population and through policy decisions. When I was young, there were about three and a half billion people on the planet, more or less. There are now eight billion. In order to feed these eight billion people, agricultural and grazing land has to increase. As it increases, the amount of forest and other land available to wild animals decreases. Although estimates are that the human population increase will eventually level off, the trends in meat-eating and related practices, as we saw a moment ago, indicate that deforestation will continue to increase.

In addition, policy decisions have allowed for deforestation of vast tracts of land. For example, in Brazil under the recent presidency of Jair Bolsonaro, deforestation of the Amazonian rain forest reached record levels. As a matter of politics, it is often more popular to engage in short-sighted policies of deforestation in order to make resources available to currently existing adults, especially voting adults, than to plan for the future of people who don't yet exist, or even the future of young children. And so population growth combined with policy decisions has led to a massive deforestation.

At this point, someone might want to throw utilitarianism into the discussion. They might say that deforestation is not so much a problem for currently existing animals but for future ones. This is because there will be less room for forest animals to thrive in, and so fewer of them will come into existence. And this would not be a problem in terms of amounts of happiness. If we assume that the decline of non-human animal births is accompanied by an expansion of human births, and hold on to the idea that humans can experience greater levels of happiness than other animals, then might there actually be an increase in overall happiness that is had by deforestation?

There are three difficulties with this way of looking at things. First, deforestation *does* have deleterious effects on currently existing animals. Deforestation limits both food sources and territorial movement for animals that now live in the forests that are being destroyed. In addition, animals with greater cognitive and emotional capacities surely notice when their living spaces are being destroyed, which will cause them fear or anxiety. We know that, for instance, elephants that have had their land restricted sometimes lash out at people or human structures, trampling them in a rage. There is no reason to believe that other intelligent animals will not notice or be affected in seeing their living space compromised, especially by large, loud machines and the invasive human shouting that goes along with them.

The second problem with the idea of substituting happier humans for probably less happy deforested animals is that it contributes to the climate crisis, which also affects the lives of currently existing animals. Many of us have seen images of starving polar bears who cannot hunt because of declining sea ice. Polar bears aren't the only ones suffering. For instance, the loss of sea ice has had devastating effects on walruses. A recent movie sponsored by *The New Yorker,* called *Haulout,* follows the work of one researcher as he documents the crowding of walruses onto land because there is no sea ice to rest on, and the consequent injury and mass death that the walrus population has endured.

Finally, regarding happiness, it is entirely unclear that an overall increase will result from the substitution. Yes, one-to-one substitution of human for animal might well result in a net gain in happiness if we buy the arguments I've given for the richness of human lives. However, deforestation is unlikely to result in a one-to-one substitution. Forests, and especially rain forests, are habitats for numerous animals of different types. Their complex ecosystems offer niches for a wide variety of species, including species (like the great apes and other primates) whose lives, as near relatives, are also capable of great richness. The likely substitution of humans for other animals through deforestation, then, is not going to be one-to-one, but instead one-to-several or even one-to-many. Therefore, the argument that deforestation, by adding humans at the expense of other animals, will result in an increase in overall happiness is at best shaky and likely false.

So it seems, then, that the utilitarian claim that deforestation will result in greater happiness really doesn't work. The human happiness that deforestation might bring is very unlikely to be greater than the suffering deforestation will cause.

But is there another way to think about this? Instead of comparing human happiness and animal suffering, perhaps we humans can act to prevent the harms that go along with deforestation? Perhaps what we need instead is environmental stewardship, that is, taking care of the land that is deforested and the animals in it? We might say that nature, after all, is a slaughterhouse, with animals constantly in search for food and in fear for their lives. By contrast, a well-tended bit of land, one cleared of predators and provided with available food, would allow the animals living on it to flourish in ways that would be unavailable to them in the natural world.

To be sure, stewarding cleared land is better than not stewarding it. Given general human attitudes toward nature, I'm not sure that we could be counted on to do much in the way of good stewardship. However, that skepticism aside, the problem with taking environmental stewardship as a substitute for deforestation is that it would only work with a limited variety of animals, specifically animals that could be domesticated. Primates, for example, don't need well-tended land; they need forests, as do African forest elephants and any number of other animals. These species have evolved to live in a forested habitat, and as a habitat changes—since forests, like other ecosystems, are themselves evolving dynamically—other species or subspecies evolve to thrive along with it. And as for the view that nature is a slaughterhouse, that is partly true, but only partly. Along with fears of predation, there seem to be moments of joy (as when young animals play together), love (as we will see), and contentment.

Isn't Nature Worse to Animals Than Humans Are?

How much of a slaughterhouse is nature? Recently, some philosophers have made the case that that "partly" is instead really "rather a lot." This raises a thorny question for the issue of continued human existence. Suppose that life in the wild is really bad, bad enough for a significant number of animals that it's in fact *worse* than life with humans, even if you include factory farming. If that's right, then not only should humanity continue to exist; in addition, we should eliminate as much wilderness as we can. Factory farming: not great, but at least it beats life in the wild.

The philosophers Kyle Johannsen and Catia Faria in their recent books *Wild Animal Ethics: The Moral and Political*

Problem of Wild Animal Suffering and *Animal Ethics in the Wild: Wild Animal Suffering and Intervention in Nature,* respectively, point out that many animals, even many sentient animals, have short, painful lives. In addition to detailing difficulties that face both adults and young offspring like predation, disease, physical injury, lack of food, and so on, they distinguish between what are called K-strategies and r-strategies of reproduction. K-strategies involve having a small number of offspring and caring for each of them carefully. Humans, in general, do that. (We all know of and often condemn the exceptions.) R-strategies, by contrast, involve having lots of offspring of which only a few are likely to survive. Those that don't survive live short, painful lives and die through starvation or predation. Johannsen believes that most sentient animals that make it to adulthood have lives worth living. However, given that there are many millions of offspring produced through r-strategies that don't make it, both he and Faria argue that the overall suffering in the wild is greater than the overall worthwhileness of life in the wild. Because of this, they believe that we should intervene in wilderness cases on behalf of animals. Think of it as stewardship on steroids.

What might this mean as we weigh human extinction? There are a couple of possibilities here. One is that human intervention into the lives of wild animals can make things better, better enough that it counterbalances the suffering we inflict on animals through factory farming, deforestation, scientific experimentation, and so on. A second, stranger possibility is that wilderness life is just so bad that we ought to do what we can to limit and perhaps even eliminate to the extent possible natural habitats.

All of this sounds, on its surface, a bit crazy, pretty much in opposition to our natural inclinations in thinking about wilderness and the environment. But it has been defended on the basis of speculating that overall suffering from human causes is dwarfed by suffering in nature, since there are so many more animals in nature that suffer than those that suffer at our hands.

What should we make of these claims? Let me offer a few responses.

First, understanding how an animal feels about its life is a tricky business. We can't just ask the animals, as we can with human beings—which was part of our response to Benatar. And we can't just assume that the struggle of animals to survive in the face of death means that their lives are good ones, since factory-farmed animals generally have terrible lives but still struggle in the face of death. Even wild animals that live short lives that end with predation or starvation might have lives worth living up until the time of death. We can't calculate the value of a life to the creature living it solely on the basis of its death or else few of us would have good lives; even a child who dies young might have a life that is both tragic and yet worth living. And, to make matters more complicated, how might we calculate the overall value of the suffering of the many losers in r-strategy reproduction as opposed to the winners? We should be leery of the proposal to eliminate entire species or habitats on the basis of evidence that is so tentative and speculative.

Second, as writers on these issues are themselves at pains to point out, intervention in the wild is itself an uncertain business. It's very difficult to tell what might be helpful and what might cause other, unexpected but disastrous consequences. Here again, the precautionary principle should hold sway. We should be as careful as we can be in intervening. However, the more careful we are, the less likely we are to eliminate the levels of suffering equivalent to those that humans cause through our other practices.

Third, a question for those who favor limiting or eliminating natural habitats. Suppose that humans had to reproduce through r-strategies rather than K-strategies. Would we then say that we should allow humans to go extinct— that there would be too much suffering in the human species to continue it? (I can't help thinking here of social media as a metaphor for r-strategies.) It's not at all clear to me that many of us would.

Fourth, there is a deontological concern here. What we considered in the first two responses is the level of suffering of animals in the wild as opposed to human-caused suffering. There is also a moral difference between these two types of suffering. Humans know what we're doing and are largely aware of the moral costs of what we do. We may not admit it to ourselves much of the time, but we are able to recognize that factory farming, deforestation, and so on are morally dubious. This is not a recognition that non-human animal predators can have. They can't ask themselves whether killing their prey is morally okay. And since they can't do that, we really can't hold them morally responsible for doing it. In that sense, regardless of the relative degrees of suffering in the wild as opposed to the suffering at our hands, we are morally responsible for that suffering in a way (or at least to a degree) that other animals are not.

Finally, the question arises of how realistic it is to expect humans to intervene on any significant scale to make the lives of wild animals better. For my part, I'm pretty skeptical that we would put significant effort into it. To be sure, recently there have been important strides made in recognizing the suffering of our fellow creatures, and some very tentative steps taken to mitigate the suffering that happens at our hands. Nevertheless, as we have seen, the overall suffering we cause to non-human animals has increased rather than decreased. Moreover, given our seeming inability to get a handle on the climate crisis, which deeply affects human life, it seems unlikely that we're going to put much effort into mitigating the suffering of various forms of prey, especially that of small animals.

So where does this leave us? We've seen that factory farming, which is on the increase, is the cause of immense animal suffering. As places like China and India expand their consumption of meat, humanity as a whole is escalating the suffering we impose upon other animals. In addition, deforestation, also on the increase, is making it more difficult for animals in the wild to conduct their lives. Moreover, there's no strong reason to believe that the suffering that other animals undergo in the wild can justify our continued existence as stewards of the environment if we continue factory farming and deforestation.

Is that it? Let's please say there is no more on this side of the ledger.

Sorry, there is more.

The Cost of Our Experiences

So far we have been focusing on the suffering that continuing human existence would create through factory farming and deforestation. There are other human practices that create suffering as well, such as the pollution of the oceans through chemical runoff, the disposal of plastic, scientific experimentation, and other practices that contribute to the climate crisis. However, since, as we have seen, there isn't a single scale for comparison, rather than listing the litany of other human practices that create unhappiness for other animals, we might rest (if that is the word) with the conclusion that it is at best unclear whether the further propagation of humanity will indeed cause more happiness than unhappiness.

Whether there is a way to address or mitigate this is a question we'll return to briefly later in this chapter and more fully in the following one. But now let's recall the second argument for carrying on with our species that we saw in the previous chapter: the idea that human existence offers important relations with the world that cannot be had by other species. It will turn out that things there are more morally complicated than we might have thought.

As we saw, humans are capable of experiences of beauty, truth, and reflectively engaging in the possibility of a good life. Other animals do not have the ability to do these things. Whether we think with Sarah Buss that art and scientific truth have independent value or with Nandi Theunissen that they have value only in relation to human beings, most of us are likely to think that these experiences are valuable. A world without them would be impoverished, and not simply because there would be less happiness. It would be impoverished by the very fact that those experiences could not happen. The world would have, as it were, zones of silence where the music of these experiences might otherwise take place.

How should we compare the value of these experiences with the pain and suffering we cause to other animals?

On the one hand, we can't really do a direct weighing. As we've seen, there isn't an adequate scale to measure the amount of happiness we add to the world compared to the amount of unhappiness. So how are we to begin to compare the value of experiences of beauty, truth, and the good life with the misery our continued existence creates?

There is an indirect approach we might take through a different type of comparison. Let's start with an imagined scenario, one that is not too far-fetched. Suppose an art museum, say the Louvre or the Metropolitan Museum of Art, were to catch fire during an exhibition. And suppose there was time either to save the art or to save the people who were enjoying the exhibition, but not both. Which would you choose to save? Obviously, the people. Even though the art from the exhibit would be lost forever, so no further experiences of enjoyment could be had from them, to argue from that to the conclusion that we ought to save the art is, I think, pretty outrageous. We would rightfully save the people.

Now imagine that rather than people in the museum during the time of the fire, there were farm animals or forest animals. That's not so likely, to be sure, but not difficult to picture either. Would you save the art or the animals? I think many of us would opt to save the animals. Our thinking might be something like this: The animals are living creatures that will suffer horrible deaths if we don't save them. The art, by contrast, won't suffer by being burned up. While it's true that nobody will be able to experience that art again, that doesn't override the suffering of those animals. Even if we agree with Buss that the art has independent value, we wouldn't use that as the basis for saying that we can sacrifice the animals for the sake of the art. We would need to save the animals and let the art go.

This, I should note, is a deontological approach to the issue. Recall that deontology is concerned not with results but with means, focusing either on intentions or rights and duties. In this case, the example is best conceived as one of rights and duties. It's not that we'd be sacrificing more happiness by saving the art rather than the animals. It's possible that we wouldn't. It might be that the happiness enjoyed by human beings over the course of their experiences of the art would outweigh the misery of the dying animals and the future happiness they would have experienced had they continued living. It's that the animals have certain rights—or, alternatively, that we have certain basic

duties toward them—that are violated if we let them die in
favor of rescuing the art. These animals do not deserve to
die so that people can continue to have enjoyable aesthetic
encounters with these paintings and sculptures.

If this is right, then at least the suffering of *some* animals
outweighs the importance of experiencing *some* art. We can't
say that *all* experiences of art justify the suffering caused to
animals.

But, someone could reply, yes, in this case it would be
better to save the animals than the art. However, that's only
because there is other art to be engaged with. The loss, for
example, of some particular paintings would be sad, especially if it was great art. Depending on your view of painting, you might say that it would be a real sacrifice if we had
to let Van Gogh's *Starry Night* or some of Rembrandt's self-
portraits burn in order to save a bunch of farm animals.
Maybe we could live with that, though. But that's because
there is other art to be seen. Even if we had to offer up all of
Van Gogh to the flames, there is still the rest of the entire
history of painting to enjoy. But what about a conflagration
that would make the entirety of, say, painting disappear?
Would we really be prepared to allow that to happen in
order to save some chickens and cows and pigs?

It is interesting to note that this example, except with
humans instead of animals, is a famous one in literature. In
Dostoyevsky's *The Brothers Karamazov,* Ivan is challenging
his religious brother Alyosha's acceptance of the world that
God has created. In this challenge, he asks Alyosha whether
he would be willing to agree to the suffering of an innocent

child if that were the price to be paid for an otherwise perfect world. To make the case vivid, Ivan offers up examples of such suffering: parents who flog their daughter mercilessly, a general who orders his dogs to tear his child apart out of pique that the kid hurt one of them, parents who make their kids sleep in outhouses, and so on. For Ivan, this suffering betrays any possibility that the world God has created is a just one. And imagining the world to be otherwise perfect would not change the case.

We could make Ivan's example more complicated if we put it in the context of the real world and asked whether, for instance, it would be acceptable to sacrifice an innocent child in order to prevent the various horrors that are daily visited upon other innocent children around the world. At some level of overall suffering we might say that the right of an innocent child not to suffer is overridden by the vast amount of suffering that would be prevented by the sacrifice. This is not an uncommon view among deontologists, most of whom agree that rights can be overridden in extreme situations.

What Ivan is getting at, however, is not a comparison between the suffering of an innocent child and overall suffering, but instead the price to be paid for what would otherwise be perfect. In other words, the scale to be balanced is between the suffering of an innocent child and a world where everything is wonderful. In the scenario we're currently imagining, the choice would be between an innocent child and the entire history of painting or the works of Shakespeare or, a little further afield, the world of baseball or soccer. How many innocent children's suffering would we be willing to countenance to save one of these?

My own view is that the number would be zero. I can't imagine allowing an innocent child to suffer greatly for the sake of preserving any of these works. I don't think I'm alone in this. And I recognize, as I write this, that this makes me a hypocrite. I do things like go out to restaurants for dinner or visit museums or watch sports when donating the money I spend on those things could save an innocent child from suffering. It's the distance from the suffering that allows this hypocrisy. If the innocent child were presented to me and I had to choose between their suffering and, say, my meal, I would, like almost all of us, skip the meal. Likewise, if directly presented with the option of saving the works of Shakespeare or allowing an innocent child to suffer, I would allow the Shakespeare to disappear. And again, I don't think I'm alone in this.

Where does this take us regarding the weighing of animal suffering versus the experiences Buss and Theunissen argue give value to humanity?

If you share my intuitions, then the loss of experiences of beauty, truth, and the good life would seem justifiable in the face of innocent suffering. We might press the point by asking whether *all* of those experiences could justifiably be sacrificed in favor of the saving of an innocent child from suffering. That's a difficult question. I would likely come out in favor of saving the child, although I recognize that not everyone would. (Here, some people might say that the experience of art can make us more humane and therefore

save more innocent children in the future. Perhaps.) However, we can at the very least recognize that sacrificing a
lot of these experiences would be a worthy price to pay to
prevent that suffering. Otherwise put, although the sacrifice of experiences of beauty, truth, and the good life would
be a tragedy, that tragedy might be overridden by the suffering that would be prevented by allowing the sacrifice to
happen.

In this case, of course, we're considering the suffering of a
fellow human being, a child to be exact. However, our bigger question here doesn't concern the suffering of innocent
human children, but instead non-human animals. If we
substituted the suffering of non-human animals for that of
children, would we have the same intuitions?

I suspect that in a one-to-one substitution, we would not.
If you asked me whether I would be willing to allow a single cow or pig to suffer to save all of Shakespeare, I would
likely say yes. As with the example of the museum, I could
let *Hamlet* or *Romeo and Juliet* go to save the creature, but all
of Shakespeare would be a pretty big ask. (To be honest, if
you asked me about *King Lear,* I would have more trouble
but would in the end probably agree to saving the animal.)

It seems to me, though, that asking this on the basis of a
one-to-one substitution is a mistaken approach. The equivalent to the life of an American is, as we have seen, nearly
two dozen pigs, more than fifteen hundred chickens, and
over five dozen cows. That's a lot of suffering to stack up
against the experiences of art or sport. Still, though, somebody might make the case that it's worth animals suffering

to ensure that experiences of the kind that humans are capable of remain on the planet: truth, beauty, the good life. That seems at least arguable.

However, that's not all of it. For the existence of these experiences to justify our continuing, we would have to weigh them against not just the amount of animal suffering caused by a single person, but the amount of suffering caused by all the human beings that will come into existence if we continue living as we do. Of course, nobody knows how many human beings will come into existence or what their eating habits are going to be in the future. Given what we do know, though, we can recognize that it will likely be an enormous amount of suffering inflicted on other animals. We've seen the annual numbers of pigs, cows, and chickens slaughtered in the United States. That's in one country in one year and solely in the practice of factory farming. The amount of suffering humans inflict on animals is astronomical. It is *that* that we would have to put on the other side of the scale, weighing it against the value of experiences of art, science, sports, and so on, in sorting out whether to go extinct.

There may well be people who would not balk at such a sacrifice, and, as I have said, the loss of such experiences would indeed be a tragedy for the world. That there would be nobody, post our extinction, to create or experience music or painting or sports or to discover scientific truths would, to my mind, impoverish the planet. Moreover, I don't have an argument to convince someone that it would be worth sacrificing those experiences to prevent that degree of suffering. There is no common measure here that would allow us to say one way or another whether the suffering is worth it. We might put the question we're confronting this way: Is the duty we owe to other animals not to cause them great suffering overridden by the good of the world's containing certain experiences? Whichever way we come down on this issue, there is an enormous amount of suffering that is to be generated in order to salvage the continued existence of the experiences associated with truth, beauty, and the good life.

But What About Love?

In the previous chapter, we raised a question about a different kind of experience—that of love—which I have put off until now. We brought up love in the context of valuable experiences, like that of art and science and sports, that are relational—that is, it is not simply a person's subjective experience of these things that is valuable, but the way each of these is engaged with by people. There are ways of being involved with the world—ways that include but go beyond a person's subjective experience—that contribute valuable dimensions to the world, and it would be tragic if they no longer existed. Among these, certainly, love surely must be counted—it would be a real loss if love were to disappear from the world with our extinction.

And yet if we count love as contributing to the world, we must ask: Are other animals capable of it? And if they are, wouldn't we have to admit that our exit would not mean the end of love in the world?

Discussions of love in philosophy are—unsurprising—varied, complex, and often in disagreement with one another. (In philosophy, almost *everything* involves disagreement. So you can imagine what happens when philosophers start talking about love.) A full treatment of the issue is far beyond the scope of what we can hope to accomplish here. To get at least a broad grip on the matter, we can start by distinguishing, on the one hand, love as a type of emotion and, on the other, love as a type of bond between people. If we focus on the idea of love as an emotion or personal experience, a number of philosophical accounts of the nature of love would seem to preclude many non-human animals from experiencing it. For instance, the philosopher David Velleman, whose writing on love is in the Kantian tradition, sees love as a deeply felt awareness of the rationality of another person. (Remember, Kant = reason.) For Velleman, love occurs when another person's rational being grips me, takes hold of me in an arresting way. This would seem to preclude most other animals on both sides of the equation. From the side of the lover, the cognitive ability to recognize reason in another creature is a high-level one. And, of course, in order for it to be recognized, there must be on the side of the beloved a rationality capable of being recognized.

Even among less cognitively oriented accounts of love as an emotion, there is a tendency to privilege human experience. Another philosopher, Bennett Helm, argues that love involves having emotions that are often felt for oneself, such as pride or gratitude or resentment, on behalf of another person. In Helm's account, even though rationality does not occupy a center role, love still requires a set of advanced cognitive abilities. This is not to say that all such abilities are strictly human. But it is surely the case that humans are capable of these emotions to a much more complex degree than other animals. So Helm's account may also preclude animals from experiencing the emotion of love as he sees it.

If we turn to the idea of love as a relation, though, things look a bit different. Accounts of love between people focus on the significance of the relationship itself, whether between lovers or between parents and children. We can see relationships within groups of non-human animals that would surely count as love or something very much like it. It is perhaps unsurprising that dolphins, who are cognitively advanced, seem to express love. Dolphins will often protect the vulnerable members of their group from shark attacks. They care for their young, as was shown when a mother dolphin was observed carrying her dead offspring on her back out to sea. Moreover, there are numerous instances of dolphins forming bonds with human beings. We might not want to call these bonds love, but they seem to indicate that dolphins can form significant emotional relationships with others that are not even of their own species.

Love as a relationship is also often associated with vulnerability to grief. Because of that, we can appeal to the classic case of elephant grief rituals as expressions of love for the deceased. Elephants will often circle around a dead member, silently running their trunks along its skin and even carrying its tusk away with them or piling soil on the dead elephant. In one observed case, as other members of the

elephant group moved on after their ritual, a single
elephant—the son of the deceased—stayed behind and kept
stroking the corpse with its trunk.

Dolphins and elephants are not close evolutionary relatives
of ours. It's not unexpected to find, then, that among the
great apes, who *are* evolutionarily closer to us, there are expressions of what seems to be love, both among adults and for
their young. Chimpanzees who share food have been found to
have elevated levels of oxytocin, a hormone associated with
feelings of love. And here is an excerpt from a story by activist
Sheri Speede about the affection between two chimpanzees,
Dorothy and Nama, that had spent many years chained in a
hotel that used them as displays for patrons' entertainment:

> Eventually, Cameroon authorities, with technical assis-
> tance from my colleagues and me, carried out a dramatic
> armed confiscation that freed Dorothy and Nama from
> their chains. The two chimpanzees had been able to see
> each other from a distance for years, but until rescued,
> they had not been able to touch. At our forested sanctuary,
> they could hold each other in sweet embraces and mutu-
> ally groom, that most important chimpanzee social behav-
> ior through which loving relationships, as well as political
> alliances, are formed.
>
> While Nama was a shining star who thrived in a larger
> social group, Dorothy's path was much more difficult.
> Four decades of isolation and strict confinement had left
> her physically frail and socially awkward. Lacking any
> self-confidence, she was an easy target for bullies. Fortu-

nately, until Dorothy found her own strength, courageous Nama kept her safe.

Ultimately, Dorothy's love for a mischievous chimp child transformed her. She had never had the opportunity to be a mother, but she became one in her forties when she adopted a young orphan we called Bouboule. In asserting herself to protect her adopted son, she gained the status and respect she had never known.

Dolphins, elephants, chimpanzees. But how about farm animals, and specifically the kinds of farm animals that are subject to factory farming? Do they express anything that could be called love? And if they do, are we humans actually inhibiting love relationships through factory farming?

It appears that, indeed, farm animals do have love relationships. There is a recent and remarkable film, *Gunda*, that follows animals on several farms, simply training the camera on them in their daily lives. *Gunda* is a film that takes a little patience; there is no music and no dialogue. It's simply a matter of watching the animals as they go about their days. Among the animals is a pig with her young. We see the young as infants and then later as they grow into early maturity. Near the end of the film (spoiler alert), the only humans who appear in the film show up. Their role is to cart off the mother pig's offspring, presumably for slaughter. This happens while she is asleep. When she awakens, she searches, with obvious increasing anxiety, for the offspring. And when she can't find them, she settles into what appears to be a form of grief or despair.

Interpreting non-human animal behavior is a tricky business. We can't ask these animals what they're feeling or how their relationships are going but can only judge by way of interpretations based on our own behavior and understandings of human interaction. However, if the question is whether experiences of something like love would go missing were humans to go extinct, we have at least some evidence that there are relationships among other animals that would count as offering the world types of richness that could more or less substitute for it.

This might not be enough for folks who want to defend human love as unique and special and therefore an important contributor to the goodness of the world. They could reply that even if we ascribe relationships of something like love to non-human animals, those relationships do not have the depth or dimensions of love relationships among human beings. Other animals cannot offer words or gifts of love in the same way. They can't consider the vulnerability or eventual mortality of their loved ones or write bad poetry to one another. Folks who think that love requires these sorts of activities and beliefs will likely also think that love involves a more nuanced emotional state than most animals are capable of. For instance, Helm's idea that love involves pride or resentment or gratitude on behalf of another can be part of a love relationship. Those emotions are unlikely to appear—or at least appear as fully—among and between animals of other species.

This marks, so far as this non-biologist can tell, a limit or near-limit to love among animals of other species. And it would be a loss if it were to disappear. However, at this point we're not talking about the total loss of something like love if humans were to go extinct. Rather, we're saying that certain expressions or dimensions of love would no longer be there. And so the weighing that would occur in this case would not be between the total disappearance of love from the world and the suffering that humans inflict on other animals, and in particular on animals that are capable of love themselves. Instead it would be the loss of particular aspects of love weighed against that suffering. Although there is no common measure between the two elements that would allow for a calculation of which is worse, there is much less of a loss with human extinction than there would be if love were to be withdrawn from the world altogether. If we made our exit, there would still be love in the world, just not the kind of love that humans experience.

Moreover, there is in both human and non-human animal love something that seems to me central to the experience. It is what the philosopher Christopher Grau calls the irreplaceability of the object of love. When we love someone, it is that particular person or animal we love. They cannot be substituted for with another similar creature. If we were told, in an imagined case, that our loved one has passed away but that another being indistinguishable from them— same appearance, same memories, same style, and so on— were being crafted for our benefit, our relation to the substitute being would not be the same as to the original. In the relationship to the original loved one, there is a shared common history that the new creature—even if they

were to be implanted with fake memories of that history—
would not have shared with us. In love, the objects of our
love are irreplaceable. That aspect of love, the fact that my
care is directed toward this particular being and not another, is something that, as we can see from our examples, is
common not only to human beings but to other animals as
well. So even if some aspects of human love were to disappear with us, the centrality of love as a relation to a particular other being would continue to exist.

The Value of Ecosystems

There is, at this point, something else worth considering,
although it's admittedly controversial within philosophical
discussions of environmental ethics. It is the value of ecosystems themselves. If ecosystems have a value, an importance
or a significance, beyond their usefulness to us and the animals that inhabit them, then our ongoing destruction of
these systems would be another consideration in favor of
human extinction. Our continuing to exist would be a
threat to things—ecosystems—that are important in themselves. So we must ask: Do ecosystems have importance?
And if so, what kind of importance do they have?

We saw in the previous chapter the distinction between
good-for and good-in-itself—that is, between something's
being good for something and something's being good just
on its own. Regarding ecosystems, there are those who
argue that ecosystems are good only in their relationship to
the plants and animals that occupy or utilize them. That is,

ecosystems are not good-in-themselves, but only good for their inhabitants or for us because of the resources they provide—shade, plants with medicinal qualities, the pumping of oxygen into the atmosphere, and so on. The idea that a system, above and beyond the living members that occupy or utilize it, might be good-in-itself, seems counterintuitive to many. Others will defend the goodness of ecosystems on their own.

There is an analogy here with species. Some people argue that species have an importance above and beyond their individual members. It might be acceptable, for instance, to hunt deer, but if deer were altogether to disappear from the planet, that would be a loss. The reason it would be a loss is that it is good that there are deer in the world—that is, that the existence of deer species is good-in-itself. That goodness does not simply lie in what deer provide in terms of food or beauty or as an ecological niche. Others who disagree but who hold a view that individual deer should be respected would argue that there is no loss of something important if deer species were to disappear, but that particular currently existing deer should not be ill-treated.

Ecosystems, then: good-in-themselves, good-for, or something else?

Let me start with a brief story. I am fortunate enough to live in western North Carolina, surrounded by the Blue Ridge Mountains. Every fall, the tree canopies gradually turn into magnificent harmonies of colors. They are practically everywhere I turn. Several months ago I was driving on a highway that led through the mountains. I was particularly struck by the fall colors and I felt a strong sense of peace at the possibility that, after I die, these mountains would continue their annual ritual of leaves turning, then falling, then reappearing in the spring. The philosopher Elizabeth Anderson uses the term "wonder" in relation to ecosystems, which seems to capture something important. Wonder is a difficult emotion to describe. We might say that it's what we feel when we come across something that seems greater and more beautiful than what we're capable of creating. What I was feeling was similar to wonder, but a bit beyond it. It was a sense of tranquility stemming from the possibility that even when I was gone, that ecosystem or its evolutionary equivalent would likely still be there. And because I was also considering the themes of this book, it occurred to me that there might be something to be said for the turning of the leaves—and the whole ecosystem of which this turning is a moment—even in the absence of anybody to appreciate it. That is, the existence of this ecosystem, apart from any of its effects on viewers or on the creatures it sustains, struck me as being important, as being good-in-itself.

This, as you'll recall, is what Sarah Buss says about things like art and science that provide the material for the instrumental value of people who can appreciate them. And, as we also saw, Nandi Theunissen took issue with this, arguing that the good of such things was in relation to human beings. I am generally sympathetic to Theunissen's view, but in this case want to suggest that there might be an exception. I have no argument for this that is likely to convince a skeptic, but let me offer the following as a sort of defense.

Creations of art and science are mostly inorganic. They are not living things. I suppose that one can create art out of living things, but for the most part standard art objects like paintings, sculpture, music, and so on, are not alive. (Even ballet and theater, which are performed by live people, are rooted in inorganic choreography and scripts.) Neither are the discoveries of science. Ecosystems, on the other hand, are networks of living creatures that evolve over time. To be sure, an ecosystem can evolve to such a point where it might become a different ecosystem. Ecosystems are, after all, dynamic and changing rather than existing in some static balance. That's just part of their evolution. There seems to me to be something to be treasured in these systems, and treasured above and beyond the admiration that they elicit in us. The entire evolving network itself is a marvel of nature, a marvel that we can appreciate but that does not need our appreciation in order to be the marvel it is.

Humans, as has often been recognized, are a threat to many ecosystems. Although we are inseparable from nature, our history is one of seeking to subdue and often destroy the nature of which we are a part. The climate crisis in particular, which is our doing, is a threat to many ecosystems, from the Brazilian rain forest to the Australian coral reefs. Might one reason not to continue our existence as a species, then, be that it would preserve certain goods-in-themselves—these networks of living beings that are threatened by our practices?

This will certainly not be convincing to those who aren't impressed by the idea that an ecosystem can be good-in-itself. However, even those who might be sympathetic to the general idea would point out that there is a certain weighing that must be done here. Wouldn't we have to weigh the good of the ecosystem itself against the good of continued human existence, with all the happiness and the experiences that humanity contributes?

We would, but there is one difference. Ecosystems are networks of currently existing living creatures. What we would be weighing, then, is the goodness of humans that aren't here but will come to exist against the goodness of currently existing networks of creatures. Why? Because the goodness of the humans who come to exist will be at the expense of those networks of creatures. And here we can say something in favor of the networks.

For instance, most of us believe that we owe something to currently existing humans, some basic respect, however that is conceived. (We're never far from Kant and his concept of dignity, are we?) We also owe something to future human beings, *assuming they will come to exist*. However, let's imagine that the only way to respect currently living people would be not to produce any future ones. Imagine, for instance, that bringing more people into existence will create such a stress on the food system that currently existing people would starve. Then we shouldn't create more people. We don't owe it to future generations to create them. Remember, there is no particular "them" that we are obliged to create.

Something analogous seems to be the case with ecosystems, as long as we recognize them as good-in-themselves. The protection of a currently existing good-in-itself strikes me as generally more important than the production of something that will be a good-in-itself in the future (or, taking Theunissen's view, a good-for-itself), when the creation of the latter is a threat to the former. There may be exceptions to this, but it seems like a good rule of thumb. If so, then the protection of ecosystems from human beings who do not exist but would pose a threat to them may well override the production of those further human beings.

Scheffler and the Loss of Meaning

We have looked at three reasons for not continuing human existence: the unhappiness we produce over and against the happiness we would contribute; the misery we create over and against the experiences of truth, beauty, and the good life; and, briefly, the threat we pose to ecosystems. We have not posed anything against Scheffler's point that continuing humanity in general is important for currently existing people. I don't believe there is anything else to add on that point. Recall that Scheffler's defense of human continuity focuses not upon future humans but on currently living ones. Unlike the issues of happiness and valuable experiences, he is not weighing future possibilities but the effect of future possibilities on present living humans. That is, if there were to be no more humans in the future, that would sap some of the meaningfulness of current human lives, in ways that we have seen.

However, there is a challenge to what some might consider the implications of Scheffler's view that we can raise: Is the suffering that our continued existence would produce in other living beings (and, if one values these, the harm to ecosystems) outweighed by the importance to currently existing humans of the continuity of our species? Is the harm brought on by factory farming, deforestation, the climate crisis, pollution, and so on—is this all worth it to ensure that the lives of currently existing people are more fully meaningful—for instance, that projects oriented toward the future have a chance at being realized?

As always, there is no scale on which to weigh this. But also, as with experiences of truth, beauty, and the good life, it seems to me very much a live question of whether the suffering we cause is worth the meaningfulness provided by human continuity. I believe that Scheffler is right that the existence of future humans contributes in an important way to the meaningfulness of many of our lives. But I also believe, as does Scheffler, that it is not the only thing that contributes. The meaning of the lives of many of us would be diminished if there were no future generations, in some cases diminished significantly, but it would not be entirely extinguished. So what we would have to weigh here is the meaningfulness that would be lost if humanity ended over and against the misery and loss that would be prevented if we did end. There is not, it seems to me, a clear answer as to how to weigh these. And, for our purposes, it does not seem obvious that however we do weigh these, the scale will necessarily tilt toward the creation of future generations of humans.

A Smaller Population—Redux

Finally, let's turn, as we did in the previous chapter, to the question of much smaller human populations. We saw there that much of what is good about the continuation of humanity would still be in place in a smaller population of people. How about this, then: Could the harms our future existence would cause be mitigated through a much smaller population?

Well, the fewer humans there are, the fewer animals will be mistreated for the sake of our nourishment, especially our nourishment through factory farming. In addition, there would be less deforestation and pollution, a smaller carbon footprint, and fewer ecosystems threatened. All of this would mean less harm from our continued existence.

But would a smaller population of humans, although causing less misery, still cause more misery than if we did not continue to exist at all?

We can imagine a situation where that might not be the case. Suppose a smaller population were to exist. It would be less likely that it would need practices like factory farming. Instead, with our current knowledge, animals could be raised and slaughtered humanely. They would have good lives until they died, which would contribute happiness to the world; and, of course, it would be good for them if they existed. (We should be careful here. It would not be good for them *to be brought* into existence, since there is no "them" before they come to exist. It would be good for them to exist once they came into existence.) Along with this, we could imagine agricultural practices that are more sustainable and, again with current knowledge, recycling practices that limit the amount of plastic that destroys the oceans. All of this accords with the environmental stewardship we saw briefly a bit ago. A limited population would also put fewer greenhouse gases into the atmosphere. In all, it might seem possible that a smaller population, say of a few million or maybe even a billion or so people, might carry on the goods of human existence without threatening to create more misery than we're worth.

That is the potential upside. But would that population eventually grow again? The history of humanity is, at least since the agricultural revolution, one of expanding populations. As a species, we tend not simply to reproduce ourselves but to increase our numbers. I suppose there are good evolutionary explanations for that, hedging as it does against infant mortality and other hazards of human existence. And, after all, there are good non-evolutionary reasons for engaging in the activity that increases populations. For whatever reasons, where there are humans there seem to come more humans, often lots more. If this is the case, then a small human population won't remain so small. And if it doesn't remain so small, then we face the threat of re-creating the problems we hoped that a smaller population would solve.

Is it necessary that human populations will increase? I don't think so. There are two factors that could tell against it. First, we know that providing access to education and other routes of independence for women, in addition to its other benefits, is also the most effective form of birth control. In a smaller population of gender equality, then, there is less likelihood of gradual population expansion. Second, we know how to prevent infant mortality and other ills that beset humanity. On the one hand, this might contribute to expanding the population; but on the other, it might induce a smaller population to preserve the lives of its currently existing members, particularly if those lives are flourishing ones. All this, of course, is quite speculative. But when it comes to moral considerations about our future existence, speculations of this sort are unavoidable. In fact, they are to be welcomed if we hope to get a grip on this difficult issue.

Okay. This chapter has been a rough ride. It's not easy confronting the fact that we as a species have caused such massive suffering in so many ways to our fellow creatures. But there are lessons for us here, lessons that, should we take them up, would make our continued existence more justifiable, or at least more nearly justifiable. Let's turn now to those lessons, then. How should we as a species proceed so as not to be a blight (or so much of a blight) upon the earth?

FOUR

Where Does This Leave Us?

WE HUMAN BEINGS HAVE SOME good reasons to continue our existence. We bring a lot of happiness into the world. We are capable of a variety of experiences that are unavailable to other animals. Continuing our existence is an important contributor to the meaningfulness of people who are currently alive. We also have some good reasons not to continue, reasons that are tied up with the massive suffering we inflict on other animals and the destruction we cause to the world's ecosystems.

Should we go extinct? After following the twists and turns of the previous chapters, it's difficult to come down clearly on one side or the other. But that in itself should be disturbing. Realizing that whether our continued existence is morally justified is a live question is alarming to me, and I suspect it would be to many of you as well.

But we need not become hostages of our alarm. We can use it to mobilize ourselves to make the world better, to end or at least minimize the suffering we cause to other animals. We might ask ourselves what lessons we can draw for molding our future existence in order to make it more—or at least more nearly—justifiable. In this chapter, we will look at some of those lessons, regarding food, deforestation, population, the climate crisis, scientific experimentation, and our attitude toward nature and other animals.

Before we do, however, let's take a moment to consider a current popular moral approach that, to my mind, exemplifies what is wrong with the way we humans so often think about our future on the planet. It provides a helpful jumping-off point for the lessons we actually do need to take on board in looking at our future.

Longtermism

Recently, a moral approach to the future of humanity has been enjoying a moment of publicity rarely accorded to philosophical theories. Longtermism, a term coined by William MacAskill, has been endorsed by the likes of Bill Gates and Elon Musk, and MacAskill's recent book *What We Owe the Future* has appeared on the *New York Times* bestseller list. To understand the ideas behind longtermism, we need to understand its root in the Effective Altruism movement. And to understand that, we need to turn to a 1972 essay by Peter Singer, "Famine, Affluence, and Morality."

In philosophy, one way of giving life to an idea is to have a striking image associated with it. Singer's striking image, which has had lasting influence not only in philosophy but in the wider public imagination, is that of his essay's drowning child. Imagine you see a child drowning in a shallow pond. You can save the child, but at a minor inconvenience to yourself—you'll ruin your shoes or get your pant cuffs wet. Is it okay to appeal to those inconveniences as an excuse to forego saving the child? Of course not. You are obliged to wade in there and save the kid. Moreover, it's not an act of charity if you do; there's nothing to praise about it. It's your obligation, according to Singer.

Now suppose you could save a child in a foreign country by writing a small check. That's inconvenient, too. (Maybe we can Venmo?) But is it any different from saving the child in front of you? Does it require any greater effort on your part? For Singer, it doesn't. Further, if saving the drowning child is an obligation, then so is writing the check. Distance is morally irrelevant here. The fact that that child lives far away while the drowning child is right in front of you does nothing to change the moral character of the situation. And you don't deserve any more praise for writing the check than you do for saving the child. It's just something you ought to do. In Singer's article, the focus, as the essay's title hints, is on giving to famine relief, although that is just an example of where someone might donate their time or money.

If this is right, where does all this giving end? For Singer, in principle it should end when you're in roughly the same position as the person you're helping. That, for him, would be the situation of greatest overall utility. However, Singer recognizes that he's asking more than almost anyone would be willing to give, and he offers a fallback principle of giving until you would have to sacrifice something of moral significance. So, for example, you probably should donate the tuition you would pay for your kids to go to an elite university rather than attend the local public college, but you wouldn't have to donate the tuition for the local public college.

From this example and Singer's analysis of it arose the Effective Altruism movement. (Yes, that's the movement that Sam Bankman-Fried appealed to in his "work," although I think it's fair to say that he did not entirely conform to all of the movement's tenets.) The idea behind the movement is that people ought to give what they can to benefit those in need in the most effective way. The question is always: What's the most effective way to create good in the world—that is, what kind of giving will cause the most overall good?

There are two sides to consider when it comes to this giving. On one side, there is the recipient. Some recipients will receive a lot of good through donations, but others not so much. Donating to a theater troupe might create some good, but donating money for mosquito nets that will prevent malaria will do much more good. (We can think of the idea of "good" here as like the utilitarian concept of pleasure or happiness, only a bit wider.) On the other side is the donor. What can the donor do to be in a position to create the most good? For Singer, doing things like taking a high-paying but alienating job on Wall Street that would allow you to donate lots of money is a worthy life pursuit, as is being prepared to give a kidney to save someone who might otherwise die.

However, the Effective Altruism movement is not without its critics. Some are uncomfortable with the counsel to offer charitable donations when perhaps political change is called for and might, in the end, be more effective. The movement largely ignores sticky political issues, although that's not necessarily entailed by its philosophical framework. Relatedly, others have questioned whether charity actually reinforces current political structures by relieving them of their obligation to assist their own citizens, or even winds up supporting corrupt regimes that might otherwise face more determined popular resistance.

Recently, however, some in the Effective Altruism movement, MacAskill among them, have questioned whether it is more effective to donate to people who currently exist or instead to ensure that the environment for future people is a safe one. After all, they argue, there will be vastly more people who will come to live on the planet than are living now, likely vastly more than have *ever* lived. So, they suggest, the most effective way of utilizing our resources is to make sure that the lives of those future people are good ones rather than to focus solely on the present. That is longtermism: focusing on the good of those to come in comparison with the good of those already here.

Longtermism supports some commonsense policies, like those that will mitigate the climate crisis. It can also, however, endorse some pretty wild ideas. As the philosopher Kieran Setiya points out, assuming there will be eight trillion human beings who follow us, longtermists would, by their own logic, be committed to saying that it would be better to sacrifice a million lives now to prevent an event that has a .0001 percent chance of wiping out the human race. Why? Because the happiness of those eight trillion people would swamp the happiness of the million, even if we factor in the improbability of the event itself.

In the hands of some longtermists, things get even wilder. There are those who take the position that we should be helping the already better off thrive because they're more likely to contribute to future well-being through job creation or donating or whatever; others speculate that we should engage in various forms of genetic engineering to create populations of happy people. We need not go into these ideas. What we should recognize is that, like many who are consumed by climate anxiety, longtermists focus on humanity's future while ignoring the downside of continued human existence.

But how should we think about the long term, really? Longtermism focuses almost solely on the good of humanity's future, with no real taking account of our effects on other animals. A true longtermist would approach the long term not as a set of policies but instead as a question, actually two questions: Should there be a long-term existence for humanity, and if so, what should it look like? We've been asking the first part of that question here, and are about to ask the second part. (In *What We Owe the Future*, MacAskill briefly considers our effects on non-human animals, concluding that our effects on farmed animals are increasingly worse and speculating that our effects on wild animals may be a bit better. However, he does not follow any of this out to the larger question.) And while a definitive answer is, as we have seen, elusive, there are lessons we can take up that would make our long-term existence either more or at least more nearly justifiable. Those lessons present challenges as well. Let's take a brief look at a few of them.

FOOD

The previous chapter focused a good bit on the deleterious effects of factory farming. It's an appalling practice—or set of practices. Factory farming creates staggering numbers of animals, which it then houses in overcrowded facilities, separating parents from offspring, feeding often unnatural or even unhealthful diets, and then killing early and often cruelly. There seems to be no moral justification for the existence of factory farming.

And yet, in a sense, there *is* a moral justification, at least under current conditions. To see why, let's consider what happens when people turn away from factory farming.

There are at least two ways to do that. The first is to consume only humanely raised animals. The second is to opt for veganism or a vegetarianism that only uses dairy products from humanely raised animals. Neither of these practices is easy to sustain. An immediate problem is that of distinguishing humanely from egregiously raised animals. There are currently no strict standards for labeling meat or dairy products, and so it's a simple matter to present them as more decently raised than they actually are. You'd have to do a lot of research to be confident that what you're buying is or has really come from a humanely raised animal.

The second problem is deeper. After all, with enough time it's possible to get a grip on the right products. However, overcoming the price difference between humanely raised animals and those from factory farms is a more difficult challenge for many people. There's a reason that factory farms do as well as they do. By treating animals as nothing more than objects to be mass-produced, factory farms are able to sell animals and animal products for much less than farms that offer humanely raised meats and products.

It might seem as though this problem, too, can be overcome if people are just willing to pay more for their food. For some of us—those in more fortunate financial conditions—that's a workable solution. If we can afford to buy humanely raised animals, we should. To allow animals to endure lives of suffering when one can pay a little more for humanely raised food is a serious moral deficiency.

However, there are many people for whom paying more for their food would constitute a significant burden. Inequality in the United States, as in many other places, is both stark and growing. We have billionaires who are making a hobby of paying for rides into space while others—many of them people who work for those billionaires—are living from paycheck to paycheck, if that.

Further, many of the poorest people in the United States and elsewhere live in food deserts, places that do not have an abundance of supermarkets. The few places that sell food are often overpriced, since there is no competition from other grocery stores. As a result, working and unemployed people frequently resort to fast food restaurants for their meals. Fast food, while unhealthy, is often the cheapest option for food consumption. And fast food cannot be made cheaply without a reliance on supplies from factory farms.

The challenge, then, is not simply one of abolishing factory farms. This would be difficult enough, given the lobbying that companies who own those farms can bring to bear. It is also the further challenge of ensuring that people have the resources to eat a healthful diet. This isn't just a matter for the food industry. It concerns the way wealth is spread in the United States and indeed around the world. In order to abolish factory farming without leaving large numbers of people hungry, we would need to deal with inequality at the same time as we deal with the farms themselves. That is a much larger, in fact daunting, task.

Does this mean that we are stuck with factory farms? That there is nothing individuals can do to limit the harm from factory farming? Hardly. There are two reasons to refuse to consume products from factory-farmed animals to the extent that you can afford to. First, you're probably not alone. If only one person stopped buying factory-farmed animals or their products, that would do nothing to change the number of animals subject to the mass suffering caused by these farms. However, there are likely to be many others who feel similarly and have the resources to make the same choice. As education about the horror of the practices in factory farming spreads, so does the number of people who refuse to participate in sustaining these practices. Collectively, this can have an effect on the number of animals brought into existence under such egregious conditions.

That, as you might have guessed by now, is a utilitarian argument. It concerns the amount of suffering that might be eliminated if we gave up consuming factory-farmed products. But there is another argument for abstinence as well, one that concerns the kind of person you want to be: Do you want to be someone who participates in practices of cruelty against fellow creatures or not, especially when you can afford not to? The answer to this question relates to your sense of who you are.

It's the type of question we can apply to many areas of our lives. If you've ever told someone you wanted to abstain from a practice you consider immoral, like refusing to buy products from a company that engages in massive pollution or limiting the amount of flying you do because of air travel's contribution to the climate crisis, you may have been asked, "What good will it do? You're only one person." Yet our lives are more than just vehicles for good consequences. The way each of us lives our life is important. And so asking who you want to be—in this case, in regard to animal cruelty—can be answered without always having to appeal to the way it will help the animals themselves.

However, the "you're only one person" question isn't wrong in fact. In the end, if we're going to justify the continuance of humanity overall in the face of practices of factory farming, individual abstinence will not supply that justification. Factory farming itself will have to be abolished, and in order to do that, economic inequality will have to be overcome in favor of a more equitable distribution of wealth and resources.

POPULATION

As we've already discussed, reducing the birth rate of the human population would have several positive effects on other living creatures and the ecosystems in which they live. First, it would involve less consumption of meat, and in particular of factory-farmed meat. Second, it would help mitigate deforestation and more generally the destruction of ecosystems, for several reasons. More people require more food, which in turn leads to more grazing for animals, which in its turn leads to deforestation. In addition, as population increases, so do agricultural needs, which requires the clearing of land for crop development. Finally, increases in population require more housing. These houses have to be built somewhere, either on land that is cleared for that purpose or on land that was previously used to address some other human need, which will then have to be addressed by clearing some other land.

A third positive effect of depopulation would be the resulting alleviation of the climate crisis. The existence of fewer people, by limiting deforestation, would allow more carbon to be withdrawn from the atmosphere by plants and trees. In addition, a smaller population could lead to less production and consumption, which could lower the emission of greenhouse gases. Now, these aren't *necessary* consequences of a smaller population; it is possible that a smaller population with more disposable income could make up in spending per person what it loses in spending with a larger population, and goodness knows we don't need any more Hummers on the road. However, combined with other policies that discourage overconsumption, there is reason to think that having fewer humans would produce a positive effect on the climate crisis.

Of course, the big question is: How are we to reduce the human population, which, as we have seen, has grown exponentially over the previous fifty years or so? (Granted, some studies predict a peak of human population later in the century; nevertheless, that peak is at about ten billion people). It is commonly recognized that the most effective form of population control is the education, and in general the empowerment, of women. This should not be surprising. Providing access to education for women has several effects. It keeps women of childbearing age in school longer, which limits their window for childbearing, and it gives them more career options. This in turn offers reasons to put off childbearing while they develop the skills they have attained through their education. Longer careers mean later and likely fewer children. So, alongside the goods associated with equality that promoting women's education involves, reducing population stands as a key benefit.

There are two clear challenges to expanding women's education. Countries with higher birth rates tend to be poorer and so have fewer opportunities for education and careers. There are also cultures that relegate women to secondary and even tertiary roles, and these cultures often overlap with areas of the world that are impoverished—though it would be rash to chalk up any causal relationship between the two. Ascribing poverty to the embrace of certain cultural norms would neglect, for instance, the role of colonialism in creating egregious forms of poverty in the first place.

Nevertheless, if the birth rate is to be reduced, this will require both economic and cultural changes. There will have to be a commitment on the part of economically advanced countries to countries that are less so, which would require citizens of those advanced countries to recognize the role they must play in the larger world. This is no easy ask, given the place that nationalism, racism, and just plain greed currently occupy. Promoting cultural change would have to be more delicate still. Given the legacy of colonialism, the advice from economically advanced countries to those in exploited countries to become more like those at whose hands they have been exploited and oppressed is not likely to be received kindly, and for good reason. Cultural intervention would have to be subtler, something that is done in league with those in cultures that marginalize women rather than something that is imposed upon them. So far, economically advanced countries have not had a stellar track record when it comes to cooperative projects with less developed countries.

A further challenge is that reducing the human population does not come without its own costs. In the United States, for instance, there are periodic crises associated with the funding of Social Security. As healthcare improves (a good thing, to be sure), the aging population grows larger relative to the younger one. This means that fewer people are contributing to Social Security relative to the number of people who are drawing from it, which results in fears of bankruptcy of the system and questions of how to ensure the solvency of the program. Otherwise, we would face a growing population of older folks living in poverty or near-poverty. The money for Social Security can be raised, but it would likely require funding from other resources, like taxes. And that taxation would fall on those who are funding retirees, which adds another burden to them in a time in which jobs are less secure for and often less available to young folks.

The difficulty is not confined to the United States. Any country with a system of financial support for its elderly is likely to encounter it. Moreover, even populations that don't have such a system will still face the problem of increasing numbers of elderly members relative to younger ones as long as healthcare continues to improve. And remedying this with an increase in the population of younger members, which would place less of a burden on each member, comes at the cost of expanding the population with all its attendant problems.

I would like to have a clear solution to this dilemma, but to address it adequately requires expertise in areas of economics and politics that are beyond mine. It strikes me as a real challenge, though, one that needs to be confronted if we are to limit the human population going forward and thus become more justified in *our* going forward.

DEFORESTATION

As we've been looking at different approaches to justify continuing humanity—as well as the obstacles in enacting those approaches—we've been treating each approach and its obstacles as separate elements in the larger story. However, we should recognize the interaction among these elements at three levels: their causes, their effects, and the challenges in addressing them. Deforestation provides a telling example.

Deforestation arises both in part from the pressures of supplying food and from increases in population. The need for more meat has turned forests into grazing areas, and the need for more crops has increased agricultural land at the expense of habitable land for other animals. In turn, deforestation contributes to the climate crisis we will discuss in the next section. Finally, the challenges to ending deforestation require revisiting economic inequality as well as other practices contributing to the climate crisis.

To see this more clearly, let's look briefly at one example, although a significant one—that of the deforestation of the Brazilian part of the Amazonian rain forest. As we have seen, under the Bolsonaro administration, deforestation accelerated rapidly, although it was happening before he took office. His successor, Luiz Inácio Lula da Silva, has vowed to stem the tide of deforestation, but he will face pressures to allow the practice to continue.

Deforestation of the Amazon has certain short-term economic benefits. It allows for the grazing of cattle—which is the prime cause of Amazonian deforestation—logging, and agriculture. These industries provide employment and allow for an increase in consumer goods as well as foreign trade. Brazil is still a developing country, and it could use the jobs created through these industries. The people who get those jobs are more likely to support political candidates who foster the conditions for them, leading people to endorse political leaders who embrace policies of deforestation. This likely contributed to the support Bolsonaro received in the recent presidential election, even though he was unpopular in many other ways.

Yet not only has the deforestation of the Brazilian rain forest had negative effects on the indigenous populations of the Amazon; it is a key driver of the climate crisis. The Amazonian rain forest, because of its mass and density, has been a central source of carbon sequestration—at one point, before deforestation, it was estimated to absorb 4 percent of annual worldwide carbon emissions. And yet because of the rate at which it is being destroyed, the rain forest region is currently a net *emitter* of carbon. Should deforestation continue, there will be a worsening of already deleterious effects on non-human animals. First, their habitat will continue to decrease, which will limit the resources not only of various species of animals in the rain forest that might come into existence but also of those already in existence. Second, since the climate crisis is a worldwide phenomenon, it will modify environments far from Brazil, which in turn will pressure the animal populations in those environments to adapt or die. Finally, it is destructive of an ecosystem that, as I suggested in the previous chapter, might have value in itself. In fact, there are indications that the entire Amazonian rain forest might be in danger of collapse.

Addressing the current deforestation in Brazil will not be a matter solely of prohibiting economic activity in the region. Even still, there will likely be popular sources of resistance to such economic measures, since the activities that lead to deforestation are woven into the Brazilian economy. Changing this means providing alternative opportunities for employment, which will require infusions of money into Brazil's economy. One proposal for such infusion would be to have other countries, in particular those with a history of carbon and other greenhouse gas emissions, pay Brazil to preserve its remaining rain forest areas. The reasoning behind this is that since those countries have gained economically through their own emissions, they should pay for those gains by helping to mitigate the problems they have caused.

However, this would require the populations of those emitting countries to agree to send money abroad not as an investment for which they might hope to gain an economic return, but instead to pay for something that happened in the past. If the United States' attitude is any indicator of the difficulty of doing this, it will not be easy. Dominant factions in the Republican Party have evolved from supporting addressing the climate crisis to denying that it exists. It is likely to use any policy of payment for rain forest preservation in another country as an excuse to criticize the administration whose policy it is for being unconcerned with national needs and the national interest.

The difficulties presented by the attempt to preserve the Brazilian rain forest constitute only one example of the challenges here. To be sure, it is an important example, but it is easy to imagine these challenges emerging wherever the preservation of forests clashes with short-term economic gain. The obstacles to be overcome in addressing them require not only national but international cooperation, a type of cooperation that, as the climate crisis itself shows, has not been easy to come by.

CLIMATE CRISIS

Deforestation. Desertification. Rising sea levels. Devastating heat waves. Bleached coral reefs. Collapsing ecosystems. The climate crisis has it all, with ruinous environmental effects across the planet. As we have seen, the crisis emerged not from a single cause but from multiple sources. We have noted its sources in the meat industry, population increase, and deforestation. But that is not all. In highly industrialized countries, consumer behavior—especially activities like car and air travel—contribute significantly to carbon emissions. Moreover, the crisis cannot be stemmed even if greenhouse gas emissions were to end today. The effects of those emissions are backloaded. The heat waves, flooding, fires, and storms stemming from or exacerbated by the climate crisis that we are feeling today are not the result of current emissions but of past emissions. Current emissions will compound those effects in the future, which is why the goal of the Paris Agreement of 2015 to limit the rise of global temperature 1.5 degrees centigrade over pre-industrial temperatures is now seen as extremely unlikely.

The effects of the climate crisis on humans are a source of well-founded worry. However, the climate crisis is calamitous not only for humans but for non-human animals as well. To take just one example, the bleaching of coral reefs has devastated the populations of fish that inhabit them, ending not only the individual lives of particular fish but threatening entire species.

Because of its extent and its multiple sources, it is difficult to get a grip on the moral phenomenon of the climate crisis. One helpful approach is offered by Stephen Gardiner in his book *A Perfect Moral Storm: The Ethical Tragedy of Climate Change.* Borrowing an image from Sebastian Junger's extraordinarily popular *The Perfect Storm,* a book about the convergence of three raging storms on a fishing vessel in the North Atlantic Ocean in 1991, Gardiner argues that there are three *moral* storms that converge in the climate crisis. The first is the storm of rich and poor. Those living in economically advanced countries are the major source of the climate crisis, while those in economically less developed countries (and economically less developed areas within the advanced countries) bear its brunt. The latter tend to live in low-lying areas that are vulnerable to flooding and sea-level rise or in areas with lower land values that attract large-scale polluting industries. This itself is not the moral storm, though. The storm arises because those in wealthier countries—who are benefitting economically from the production of products associated with greenhouse gas emissions while not paying the bulk of costs in terms of environmental destruction and economic loss—do not have an incentive to address the problem. The benefits of the climate crisis, at least in the short term, are flowing in the direction of the wealthier and more powerful as most of its costs flow to the poorer and less powerful.

The second moral storm is intergenerational. The beneficiaries of the climate crisis live in the current generation while those who will bear its burden are either younger or not yet alive. This is particularly true since the effects of greenhouse gas emissions are backloaded. As a result, addressing the crisis will require currently living generations to pay for mitigation even though the benefits for that payment will be enjoyed largely by those in succeeding generations.

The third moral storm is theoretical. We do not, Gardiner argues, have an adequate theoretical framework for understanding our climate obligations, especially to further generations. Currently, the dominant conceptual framework for addressing the crisis is a cost-benefit analysis, asking how much we value the climate in monetary terms and balancing that against the cost of preserving it. Cost-benefit approaches have many shortcomings, not least of which is the attempt to create monetary equivalents of the benefits of goods like enjoying the natural world, biodiversity, and living without the fear of devastating floods and heat waves. In addition, many theorists who address the question of what we owe future generations apply what is called a "discount rate." This is the idea that we can discount our obligations to further generations in favor of the current one. They argue for this for several reasons, among them the decreasing value of currency over time and a further assumption that future generations are generally better off than previous ones—an assumption that is at odds with the climate crisis itself. (We might think of this further assumption as the inverse of longtermism, which emphasizes our moral duties to succeeding generations at the expense of the current ones.)

Addressing these storms requires embracing moral commitments that are at odds with the focus on self-interest and national interest characteristic of political parties. Moreover, it requires people to consider the interests of those who are far from them in space and time: people in other countries or other areas in one's own country, as well as those who will come to exist. To grapple with these moral storms demands a shift in personal morality, especially among the privileged, as well as in political morality.

Might there be hope for the future in addressing the climate crisis? The history of climate agreements is not promising. The reluctance of industrially advanced countries to come to terms with their contribution to the climate crisis, whether through decreased oil production or consumption, paying countries not to produce greenhouse gases, or compensating countries and peoples who have suffered because of climate emissions, has stymied efforts to address the cascading effects of the warming of the planet.

There has been one change that might provide motivation for a more urgent approach, although its longer-term effect has yet to be seen. It is the increasing volatility of the climate itself, from heat waves to flooding to fire. Larger numbers of people in economically advanced countries are beginning to experience the consequences of a warming climate, which had previously been confined to less economically developed countries and areas. As Samuel Johnson once quipped, "Depend upon it, sir, when a man knows he is to be hanged in a fortnight, it concentrates his mind wonderfully."

However, how that concentration will play out is another matter. Will it lead to increasing international commitment and cooperation? Or will it instead lead to countries becoming more self-protective at the expense of an overall capacity to address the crisis itself (as happened in the United States during the Trump administration)?

SCIENTIFIC EXPERIMENTATION

I have not to this point said much about scientific experimentation on animals. Although the number of animals affected by the experiments performed on their bodies is dwarfed by factory farming and the effects of the climate crisis, it is still significant. It is estimated that more than one hundred million animals every year are subjected to scientific experimentation. The actual number is difficult to calculate, since statistics on animal experimentation are not consistently kept. It is fair to say, though, that vast numbers of animals are kept in laboratories for the purpose of experimentation on their bodies, often in painful and even life-threatening ways.

Whether it is morally permissible to experiment on animals depends largely on three factors: which animals are the subject of the experiment, what is being done to them, and what the expected benefits are of such experimentation.

Alternatives to animal testing, especially with the emergence of computer simulations, have arisen in different areas of scientific experimentation. Nevertheless, there are still areas where it is claimed that experimenting needs to be done in order to protect human life. This is a difficult moral arena to sort out. On the one hand, experimentation involves animals that are subject to debilitating and sometimes life-threatening procedures that will offer no benefit to them. On the other, if the experiments are in important areas such as cancer research, there could be enormous advantages that will derive from them. It is increasingly recognized that there are at least some animals that should not be the subject of experimentation. Those are the animals evolutionarily closest to us humans: the great apes. In fact, in 2008 the Spanish parliament approved a measure protecting the great apes from experimentation. This measure derived from an activist organization, the Great Apes Project, founded by, among others, the philosopher Peter Singer, whom we saw above in connection to Effective Altruism. His 1975 book *Animal Liberation* is often considered to have launched the modern animal rights movement.

Singer himself offered a criterion for testing on animals that is widely discussed in philosophical circles. It's founded on the concept of "moral individualism," which is the idea that every animal (including humans) should be treated in respect of its individual characteristics and interests. This contrasts with speciesism, which focuses on one's species rather than one's individual qualities and abilities. Moral individualism would count a chimpanzee's interests as having the same weight as those of a young child, say a three-year-old, who is at the same maturational level. Among the consequences of this view is that it would be unacceptable to perform a scientific experiment on a chimpanzee that one would not be willing to perform on a child at a similar maturational age. (This view also has the consequence that people with significant disabilities count for less morally than those who do not, which has earned Singer widespread criticism from disability rights activists and their supporters.)

Singer's view is, of course, not the only one afloat in discussions of scientific experimentation, and not the only approach that seeks to protect many animals from experimentation or abuse. There are views that say protection should be given to those at higher cognitive levels, views that hold that sentience is the proper criterion for rights, and views that defend the idea that species matters for moral consideration. There are views grounded in utilitarianism, like Singer's; views grounded in Kant's thought, like Christine Korsgaard's *Fellow Creatures*; and views that our callous treatment of other animals will make us more callous with one another.

To address these views would require a separate book. However, what we can recognize from this brief discussion is that some scientific experimentation on animals may well be justified, even if it only serves human purposes. Other experimentation, not so much. What is required in this area are clear policies limiting the kinds of experiments that can be performed, the kinds of animals they can be performed on, and the purposes for which they can be performed.

Unlike factory farming, scientific experimentation does not, to my mind, need to be eliminated entirely in order to help justify our continued existence. Rather, it should be restricted so that only the most urgent issues are addressed, and they are addressed in the most humane way possible in the course of experimentation. While there has certainly been progress in this area, because of the lack of oversight around the world there is much more that needs to be done. In the context of our larger question—whether humanity should continue—it seems that the very practice of scientific experimentation on animals would not constitute a reason for human extinction. However, in certain of its practices it adds to the larger concern that we are causing more suffering than is gained through our continued existence.

ATTITUDE

This final element doesn't concern any specific practices, but in a way it concerns them all. If we are to justify our continued existence, we will likely need to change our attitude toward other animals and the natural world, and probably toward one another. I am not the first person to call attention to the fact that although we are a part of nature we often act as though nature is nothing more than a set of resources for our use and enjoyment. This has been pointed out many times, but the truth of it has not yet seemed to stick.

The history of philosophy provides, sad to say, an object lesson in how not to think about animals, Jeremy Bentham and his defense of them notwithstanding. Descartes considered non-human animals to be nothing more than sophisticated machines. Kant believed that they were outside the realm of moral concern. If I tortured your cat just for fun, the wrong, Kant believed, is in how I treated you, not the suffering I caused the cat. There are still philosophers who, while opposing cruelty to animals, argue that they count for very little morally.

From our vantage point, these views might seem astonishing. After all, how can one look at an animal that has been cruelly mistreated and is in obvious pain and think that it's just a machine or that its pain doesn't count for anything morally? And yet our history is replete with examples of things that are right there before our eyes but that we nevertheless refuse to see. While I believe that the human capacity for knowingly doing evil is in general quite limited, our capacity for self-deception seems nearly infinite. And philosophers, whose job is to reflect on and raise questions about commonsense beliefs, have not been immune to this.

What would it mean to truly recognize that we are part of nature and, just as important, that there are other animals that are also part of nature and whose interests need to be respected? I think there are many ways this could happen. That recognition could be a less emotional, more cognitive or intellectual one. That is, it could involve a philosophical understanding of the place of humans and other animals in the natural world, the fact that there are important interests at stake aside from human interests, and a recognition that those interests have a moral grip on us. That understanding could be integrated into our behavior through a set of principles for action, or at least a heuristic offering guidance for a person as they navigate the world.

This approach may seem overly academic, and perhaps it is. It was my approach for a long time. Although I've taught animal rights courses for years, I did not until recently have a whole lot of empathy for other animals. I could barely stand to be around pets, and the cat that we adopted years ago lived, at my insistence, outside our house. (Do I deserve your disdain here? Yes, I do.) More recently, probably through exposure to both philosophical writings and, well, our cat, I have developed a more empathic relation to other animals. However, while helpful, I don't think it's necessary that one feel warmly toward other animals in order to recognize that they have interests and that we should respect those interests.

To be clear, recognizing our place in nature and the interests of other animals does not require that we always act so as to meet those interests. Elizabeth Anderson, whom I mentioned in the previous chapter as suggesting that wonder is a proper attitude to take toward the natural world, points out that if mice are infesting your house, it's okay to kill them. There's a conflict there between important interests of mine and those of the mice. Even if it were possible to live with the mice, their presence and remarkable capacity for reproduction would make someone's life at best very inconvenient and at some point probably unhealthy.

Even so, in dealing with a mouse infestation, it should be remembered that there are different ways to kill mice, some more painful than others. Humane mouse traps, although less efficient than poison, are a quick and far less cruel way to kill mice. I know this firsthand, having mistakenly used poison for a mouse infestation and seen a mouse crawl out of the woodwork in obvious agony. (Do I deserve some more of your disdain? Yes, I do.) After killing the mouse as quickly as I could, I realized that we should really be using the traps instead.

Whether we take a more intellectualist or more empathic approach to animals and the natural world, the central point here might be put in two very short expressions. The first one is *Other animals matter*. They matter morally; we need to integrate them into our moral considerations and moral actions. The second is *Nature matters*. I have suggested that there may be a reason to take the latter statement in the sense of good-in-itself. However, we should at least recognize that we are part of nature and that it is good for us and other animals that we respect its riches, because without it there would be none of us to do the respecting. The attitudes stemming from these two statements can vary widely in their specifics. No doubt there will be cultural influences as well as personal differences regarding their specific articulations. However, if we are to act in such a way as to justify our further existence, we will need one way or another to take these phrases on board, both in our thinking and in our lives.

Conclusion

W E HAVE LOOKED AT SEVERAL moral imperatives here: to eliminate factory farming, limit population growth, end deforestation, address the climate crisis, limit scientific experimentation on non-human animals, and develop more fitting attitudes toward other animals and the natural world.

These imperatives entail others: reversing inequality, ensuring adequate education for women, decarbonization, limiting overconsumption, reflecting on our practices, and so on.

Many of you will look at this list and agree, at least to a great extent, that these are important imperatives. However, aren't they important for their own reasons, independent of the question of human continuity or extinction? Why drag the question of the moral justifiability of our species into it? In fact, many of the imperatives here are beneficial for most human beings in addition to nature and other animals. What is the place of our larger question here?

No doubt these imperatives can be justified independent of the question of whether humanity should continue. That they have not been taken up adequately in our practices has to do with reasons that are political, cultural, economic, and social.

However, there is an aspect to the failure to embrace and act upon these imperatives that runs deeper than their effect on the lives of many of us. The stakes, it seems to me, are wider than that. Those stakes are the subject of this book. If we, as a species, cannot find a way to live in a more morally sensitive way in the world, the world might be better off without us. What is at stake is not the justification to one another of our practices, but the justification of our continuing to be here in the first place.

It will be pointed out, and rightly, that many of the failures to act on these imperatives can be laid at the doorstep of a small portion of the human population. Those of us who are economically, racially, and socially privileged have been either the causes of much of these failures or are at least their major beneficiaries. In what sense, then, does this concern the entire human species? As we have seen, though, while the root causes may be limited to only a portion of humanity, the perpetuation and expansion of these failures involves most of us. It is not simply the privileged who are engaged in deforestation or even who support policies that foster it. It is not only the privileged who benefit from scientific experimentation on other animals, often for ends that are not really necessary to us. And there is evidence that as affluence rises, so does the consumption of factory-farmed

meat. Were policies in place to prevent these practices—
policies that run counter to the interests, many of them
short term, of only some among us—then the question I've
been raising here would be moot, or at least less pressing.
But those policies are not in place, and the consequences of
that are such that a large and increasing proportion of humanity are participants in activities and practices that have
egregious consequences for other living beings with whom
we share the planet.

The stakes, then, are the moral justification of our continued existence. Not, as I have argued, the continued existence of those who are already alive. Instead, it is the
continued existence of the species itself beyond those who
now inhabit the planet. Should we bring other human beings into existence? We do no wrong to them if we do not,
because they do not already exist in some potential state.
However, if we do bring them into existence, will this mean
bringing other creatures into existence whose suffering will
outweigh the good of continued human existence? That is
the question I've been reflecting upon here. That there
probably isn't a definitive answer—at least at the moment—
and that, moreover, there are certainly elements and angles
to the question that I have neglected, does not mean that
the question is not worth asking. To the contrary, we need
to focus on the question more rigorously if we are to earn
our future existence.

Will we? Will we take necessary steps to make our future
existence morally warranted? I am not the one to say. Pre-
diction is not my strong suit. When I was in college, there

was a concert I attended with a brand-new band. The venue was so small that the band had to enter through the audience doors. I held a door open for the band members and then commented to a friend of mine that that was the closest to fame I would ever come, holding the door for a small-time rock band from New Jersey. As it turns out, it was Bruce Springsteen's band. So, no, I claim no predictive power.

But maybe that isn't even the right question. Maybe, instead of asking whether we will come to justify our future existence, we should ask instead whether we're willing to try. Instead of seeing ourselves from the outside and wondering what we'll do, perhaps we should cast our gaze inside ourselves and ask what we're willing to do. To one extent or another, we are likely to fail, or at least not reach the ideals we would set in front of us. But when it comes to our actions, the issue is not a binary one. It's not a simple question of whether or not, in the end, we can act so that our future existence is justified. Instead, we might ask ourselves—each of us alone and collectively as a species—what might better justify our continued existence on the planet. If we do not, and perhaps cannot, even know whether the continuation of humanity is overall a good thing, we do know what we can do to make it a better thing. Whether we will do that is not up to our predictive powers; it is up to our commitment. After all, who wants to wake up at 3:12 in the morning wondering whether we should even be here?

Acknowledgments

This book is, emotionally, not an easy read. It was, as well, not easy to write. Chris Grau, Kathleen May, and Ladelle McWhorter offered invaluable assistance through critical readings of early versions of the manuscript. Richard Abate, my agent, believed in the importance of the book's discussion from the beginning. I couldn't have asked for a better editor than Kevin Doughten. He labored over every line in the text, not once but four times, making numerous suggestions that improved not only the literary but also the philosophical quality of the manuscript. Amy Li's professionalism and friendliness smoothed the administrative aspects of the publication process, and Alison Kerr Miller's copyediting saved the English language from a number of my onslaughts. Mike Schur's generous introduction is more than I deserve. I am grateful to all of these folks and to you, the reader, for getting all the way to these acknowledgments.

Book and Article References, Excluding Hyperlinks

(In order of appearance in the manuscript)

Chapter One

Bentham, Jeremy, *An Introduction to the Principles of Morals and Legislation*
Mill, John Stuart, *Utilitarianism*

Chapter Two

Benatar, David, *Better Never to Have Been: The Harm of Coming into Existence*
Sen, Amartya, *Commodities and Capabilities*
May, Todd, *A Significant Life: Human Meaning in a Silent Universe*
Parfit, Derek, *Reasons and Persons*
Kant, Immanuel, *Groundwork of the Metaphysic of Morals*
Buss, Sarah, "The Value of Humanity"
Theunissen, L. Nandi, *The Value of Humanity*
Scheffler, Samuel, *Death and the Afterlife*
Scheffler, Samuel, *Why Worry About Future Generations?*

Chapter Three

Johannsen, Kyle, *Wild Animal Ethics: The Moral and Political Problem of Wild Animal Suffering*
Faria, Catia, *Animal Ethics in the Wild: Wild Animal Suffering and Intervention in Nature*
Dostoyevsky, Fyodor, *The Brothers Karamazov*
Velleman, David, "Love as a Moral Emotion"
Helm, Bennett, "Love, Identification, and the Emotions"

Grau, Christopher, "Irreplaceability and Unique Value"

Grau, Christopher, "Love and History"

Anderson, Elizabeth, "Animal Rights and the Values of Nonhuman Life"

Chapter Four

MacAskill, William, *What We Owe the Future*

Singer, Peter, "Famine, Affluence, and Morality"

Gardiner, Stephen, *A Perfect Moral Storm: The Ethical Tragedy of Climate Change*

Korsgaard, Christine, *Our Fellow Creatures: Our Obligations to the Other Animals*

Singer, Peter, *Animal Liberation*

References

Chapter One
A Disturbing Question

page 7   (In his comprehensive history of thought about
          extinction: Émile P. Torres, *Human Extinction: A History of
          the Science and Ethics of Annihilation* (Routledge, 2023).

page 16   Can they reason?: Jeremy Bentham, *An Introduction to the
          Principles of Morals and Legislation*, ed. J. H. Burns and
          H. L. A. Hart (Oxford University Press, 1970), 283.

page 16   "It is better to be a human being": John Stuart Mill,
          Utilitarianism (1879), https://www.gutenberg.org/cache/epub
          /11224/pg11224-images.html, chapter 2.

Chapter Two
What's So Good About Humanity?

page 23   Its title couldn't be more apt: David Benatar, *Better Never
          to Have Been: The Harm of Coming into Existence* (Oxford
          University Press, 2006).

page 24   "adaptive preferences": Amartya Sen, *Commodities and
          Capabilities* (Oxford University Press, 1985).

page 26   (I've written a book about this: Todd May, *A Significant
          Life: Human Meaning in a Silent Universe* (University of
          Chicago Press, 2015).

page 35   the influential philosopher Derek Parfit: Derek Parfit,
          Reasons and Persons (Oxford University Press, 1984).

page 39   the eighteenth-century thinker Immanuel Kant:
          Immanuel Kant, *Groundwork of the Metaphysics of Morals*, ed.
          and trans. Allen W. Wood (Yale University Press, 2002).

page 41   "There is nothing it is possible to think": Ibid., 9.

page 42   **An article several years back by the philosopher Sarah Buss:** Sarah Buss, "The Value of Humanity," *Journal of Philosophy* 109, nos. 5–6 (2012): 341–77.

page 42   **a recent book by Nandi Theunissen:** L. Nandi Theunissen, *The Value of Humanity* (Oxford University Press, 2020).

page 54   **In a piece in the *New York Times* . . .** followed up by two books . . . and the more technical: Samuel Scheffler, "The Importance of the Afterlife. Seriously." *New York Times,* September 21, 2013, https://archive.nytimes.com /opinionator.blogs.nytimes.com/2013/09/21/the-importance -of-the-afterlife-seriously; Samuel Scheffler, *Death and the Afterlife* (Oxford University Press, 2013); Samuel Scheffler, *Why Worry About Future Generations?* (Oxford University Press, 2018).

Chapter Three
The Other Side of the Ledger

page 64   **Here is a description of the life of dairy cows:** Factory Farm Awareness Coalition, "Factory Farming Cows: What Happens to Cows in Factory Farms?," January 4, 2022, https://ffacoalition.org/articles/factory-farming-cows.

page 66   **And here is a description of the life of pigs:** MSPC Angell, "Farmed Animal Welfare: Pigs," https://www.mspca .org/animal_protection/farm-animal-welfare-pigs.

page 69   **roughly 130 million pigs per year are slaughtered in the United States:** M. Shahbandeh, "Total Number of Hogs Slaughtered in the U.S. from 2000 to 2022," Statista, May 5, 2023, https://www.statista.com/statistics/194382 /number-of-hogs-slaughtered-in-the-us-since-2000.

page 69   **Add to that 8 billion chickens and 32 million cows:** Ema Pandrc, "How Much Chicken Does the Average American Eat a Year?" May 14, 2022, ComfyLiving, https://comfyliving.net /how-much-chicken-does-the-average-american-eat/#:~:text=1 .,in%20the%20US%20every%20year.&text=In%20other%20 words%2C%20American%20consumers,take%20some%20 readers%20by%20surprise.

page 69 **32 million cows:** M. Shahbandeh, "Number of Slaughtered Cattle in the United States from 2000 to 2022," Statista, September 13, 2023, https://www.statista.com/statistics /194357/total-cattle-slaughter-in-the-us-since-2000.

page 76 **meat consumption has been steadily rising since at least the 1990s:** Anne Grimmelt, Sheng Hong, Roberto Uchoa de Paula, Cherie Zhang, and Jia Zhou, "For Love of Meat: Five Trends in China That Meat Executives Must Grasp," McKinsey & Company, February 2, 2023, https://www .mckinsey.com/industries/consumer-packaged-goods/our -insights/for-love-of-meat-five-trends-in-china-that-meat -executives-must-grasp.

page 76 **pig-farming skyscrapers:** Guardian Staff, "China's 26-Storey Pig Skyscraper Ready to Slaughter 1 million Pigs a Year," *Guardian,* November 25, 2022, https://www.theguardian .com/environment/2022/nov/25/chinas-26-storey-pig -skyscraper-ready-to-produce-1-million-pigs-a-year.

page 77 **Poultry consumption in India:** A. Minhas, "Consumption Volume of Poultry Meat in India from 2013 to 2023," Statista, September 18, 2023, https://www.statista.com /statistics/826711/india-poultry-meat-consumption.

page 82 **humanity has deforested large areas of the planet:** Hannah Ritchie, "Deforestation and Forest Loss," Our World in Data, February 4, 2021, https://ourworldindata.org/deforestation.

page 83 **deforestation of the Amazonian rain forest reached record levels:** "Under Bolsonaro, Amazon Deforestation Hits New September Record," Al Jazeera, October 7, 2022, https://www.aljazeera.com/news/2022/10/7/under-bolsonaro -amazon-deforestation-hits-new-september-record.

page 84 **elephants that have had their land restricted sometimes lash out at people:** Brian Handwerk, "Elephants Attack as Humans Turn Up the Pressure," *National Geographic,* June 3, 2005, https://www.nationalgeographic.com/animals /article/news-elephants-attack-humans-pressure.

page 84 *Haulout,* **follows the work:** Maxim Arbugaev, *Haulout* (film), 2022, https://www.youtube.com/watch?v=8mKBZ9 dy5fQ.

page 85   **Perhaps what we need instead is environmental
             stewardship:** *Wikipedia,* s.v. "Environmental stewardship,"
             https://en.wikipedia.org/wiki/Environmental_stewardship.

page 86   **the philosophers Kyle Johannsen and Catia Faria:** Kyle
             Johannsen, *Wild Animal Ethics: The Moral and Political
             Problem of Wild Animal Suffering* (Routledge, 2021); Catia
             Faria, *Animal Ethics in the Wild: Wild Animal Suffering and
             Intervention in Nature* (Cambridge University Press, 2023).

page 88   **speculating that overall suffering from human causes is
             dwarfed by suffering in nature:** Brian Tomasik, "Habitat
             Loss, Not Preservation, Generally Reduces Wild-Animal
             Suffering," April 26, 2017, https://reducing-suffering.org
             /habitat-loss-not-preservation-generally-reduces-wild
             -animal-suffering.

page 89   **intervention in the wild is itself an uncertain business:**
             Martha C. Nussbaum, "A Peopled Wilderness," *New York
             Review of Books,* December 8, 2022, https://www.nybooks
             .com/articles/2022/12/08/a-peopled-wilderness-martha-c
             -nussbaum.

page 94   **Dostoyevsky's *The Brothers Karamazov*:** Fyodor
             Dostoyevsky, *The Brothers Karamazov,* trans. David McDuff
             (Penguin Classics, 2003).

page 100   **David Velleman, whose writing on love:** David Velleman,
             "Love as a Moral Emotion," *Ethics* 109, no. 2 (1999): 338–74.

page 100   **Another philosopher, Bennett Helm:** Bennett Helm,
             "Love, Identification, and the Emotions," *American
             Philosophical Quarterly* 46, no. 1 (January 2009): 39–59.

page 101   **dolphins, who are cognitively advanced, seem to express
             love:** "Do Dolphins Love?" Jervis Bay Wild, https://www
             .jervisbaywild.com.au/blog/dolphins-love.

page 101   **elephant grief rituals as expressions of love:** Carl Safina,
             "The Depths of Animal Grief," *Nova,* July 8, 2015, https://
             www.pbs.org/wgbh/nova/article/animal-grief.

page 102   **elevated levels of oxytocin:** Roman M. Wittig, Catherine
             Crockford, Tobias Deschner, Kevin E. Langergraber, Toni E.
             Ziegler, and Klaus Zuberbühler, "Food Sharing Is Linked to
             Urinary Oxytocin Levels and Bonding in Related and

Unrelated Wild Chimpanzees," Proceedings of the Royal
Society B (March 7, 2014), https://royalsocietypublishing.org
/doi/10.1098/rspb.2013.3096.

page 102   **Dorothy and Nama:** Sheri Speede, "What Chimpanzees
Teach Us About Love," *Wall Street Journal,* October 22, 2013,
https://www.wsj.com/articles/BL-SEB-77811.

page 105   **the irreplaceability of the object of love:** Christopher
Grau, "Irreplaceability and Unique Value," *Philosophical
Topics* 32, nos. 1–2 (2004): 111–29.

page 108   **Elizabeth Anderson uses the term "wonder":** Elizabeth
Anderson, "Animal Rights and the Values of Nonhuman
Life," in *Animal Rights: Current Debates and New Directions*,
ed. Cass R. Sunstein and Martha C. Nussbaum (Oxford
University Press, 2005), 277–98.

Chapter Four
Where Does This Leave Us?

page 117   **Longtermism, a term coined by William MacAskill:**
William MacAskill, *What We Owe the Future* (Oxford
University Press, 2022).

page 117   **turn to a 1972 essay by Peter Singer:** Peter Singer,
"Famine, Affluence, and Morality," *Philosophy & Public Affairs*
1, no. 3 (1972): 229–43.

page 120   **as the philosopher Kieran Setiya:** Kieran Setiya, "The
New Moral Mathematics," *Boston Review*, August 15, 2022,
https://www.bostonreview.net/articles/the-new-moral
-mathematics.

page 122   **currently no strict standards for labeling meat:** PR
Newswire, "USDA Urged to Strengthen Farm Animal Welfare
by Finalizing Long-Awaited Organic Standards," October 27,
2022, https://www.prnewswire.com/news-releases/usda-urged
-to-strengthen-farm-animal-welfare-by-finalizing-long
-awaited-organic-standards-301661588.html.

page 123   **Inequality in the United States:** Juliana Menasce
Horowitz, Ruth Igielnik, and Rakesh Kochhar, "Trends in
Income and Wealth Inequality," Pew Research Center,

January 9, 2020, https://www.pewresearch.org/social-trends/2020/01/09/trends-in-income-and-wealth-inequality.

page 123 **many of the poorest people in the United States and elsewhere live in food deserts:** Annie E. Casey Foundation, "Food Deserts in the United States," February 13, 2021, https://www.aecf.org/blog/exploring-americas-food-deserts.

page 127 **predict a peak of human population:** The Learning Network, "What's Going On in This Graph? | Global Population Growth and Decline," *New York Times,* November 9, 2023, https://www.nytimes.com/2023/11/09/learning/whats-going-on-in-this-graph-nov-15-2023.html.

page 127 **in general the empowerment, of women:** Missie Thurston, "Overpopulation Solutions That Put Women and Girls First," Population Media Center, June 24, 2021, https://www.populationmedia.org/the-latest/overpopulation-solutions-that-put-women-and-girls-first.

page 130 **It allows for the grazing of cattle:** Samuel Blum, Meagan Collins, Katie Hancock, Kelsey Miller, Sanjali Yadav, "Deforestation in Brazil," July 25, 2019, https://storymaps.arcgis.com/stories/38535a937f82494a8e37094d9efc6121.

page 131 **he was unpopular in many other ways:** Reuters, "Brazil's Bolsonaro Disapproval Rating Rises to All-Time High, Two Polls Show," July 8, 2021, https://www.reuters.com/world/americas/brazils-bolsonaro-disapproval-rating-rises-all-time-high-poll-2021-07-08.

page 131 **it was estimated to absorb 4 percent of annual worldwide carbon emissions:** "The Brazilian Amazon Has Been a Net Carbon Emitter Since 2016," *Economist,* May 21, 2022, https://www.economist.com/interactive/graphic-detail/2022/05/21/the-brazilian-amazon-has-been-a-net-carbon-emitter-since-2016.

page 132 **the entire Amazonian rain forest might be in danger of collapse:** Chelsea Harvey and E&E News, "Amazon Rain Forest Nears Dangerous 'Tipping Point,'" *Scientific American,* March 8, 2022, https://www.scientificamerican.com/article/amazon-rain-forest-nears-dangerous-tipping-point/#:~:text

=With%20enough%20time%20and%20forest,scale%20
drying%20across%20the%20region.

page 134   **the goal of the Paris Agreement of 2015:** David Wallace-
Wells, "Beyond Catastrophe: A New Climate Reality Is
Coming into View," *New York Times,* October 26, 2022,
https://www.nytimes.com/interactive/2022/10/26/magazine
/climate-change-warming-world.html.

page 134   **One helpful approach is offered:** Stephen M. Gardiner,
A Perfect Moral Storm: The Ethical Tragedy of Climate Change
(Oxford University Press, 2011).

page 136   **The history of climate agreements is not promising:** UN
News, "Countries' Climate Promises Still Not Enough to
Avoid Catastrophic Global Warming," October 26, 2022,
https://news.un.org/en/story/2022/10/1129892.

page 137   **As Samuel Johnson once quipped:** Morality Quotes: The
Samuel Johnson Sound Bite Page, https://www.samueljohnson
.com/mortalit.html.

page 137   **more than one hundred million animals:** Humane Society
International, "About Animal Testing," https://www.hsi.org
/news-resources/about.

page 138   **the Spanish parliament approved a measure protecting
the great apes:** Lee Glendenning, "Spanish Parliament
Approves 'Human Rights' for Apes," *Guardian,* June 26,
2008, https://www.theguardian.com/world/2008/jun/26
/humanrights.animalwelfare.

page 138   **His 1975 book:** Peter Singer, *Animal Liberation: A New
Ethics for Our Treatment of Animals* (Random House, 1975).

page 139   **views grounded in Kant's thought:** Christine M. Korsgaard,
Fellow Creatures: Our Obligations to Other Animals (Oxford
University Press, 2018).

About the Author

TODD MAY is the author of eighteen books of philosophy. He was one of the original philosophers asked to contribute to the *New York Times* philosophy blog *The Stone.* He was also one of the philosophical advisors to the hit NBC sitcom *The Good Place* and showrunner Michael Schur's *New York Times* bestselling book *How to Be Perfect.* He teaches philosophy at Warren Wilson College.